T0318527

Cambridge Elements ≡

Elements in the Problems of God
edited by
Michael L. Peterson
Asbury Theological Seminary

THE PROBLEM OF DIVINE ACTION IN THE WORLD

Joel Archer
Duke University

Shaftesbury Road, Cambridge CB2 8EA, United Kingdom

One Liberty Plaza, 20th Floor, New York, NY 10006, USA

477 Williamstown Road, Port Melbourne, VIC 3207, Australia

314–321, 3rd Floor, Plot 3, Splendor Forum, Jasola District Centre, New Delhi – 110025, India

103 Penang Road, #05–06/07, Visioncrest Commercial, Singapore 238467

Cambridge University Press is part of Cambridge University Press & Assessment, a department of the University of Cambridge.

We share the University's mission to contribute to society through the pursuit of education, learning and research at the highest international levels of excellence.

www.cambridge.org
Information on this title: www.cambridge.org/9781009475853

DOI: 10.1017/9781009270328

First published 2023

A catalogue record for this publication is available from the British Library

ISBN 978-1-009-47585-3 Hardback
ISBN 978-1-009-27033-5 Paperback
ISSN 2754-8724 (online)
ISSN 2754-8716 (print)

The Problem of Divine Action in the World

Elements in the Problems of God

DOI: 10.1017/9781009270328
First published online: November 2023

Joel Archer
Duke University

Author for correspondence: Joel Archer, jvarcher@gmail.com

Abstract: The world's major monotheistic religions share the view that God acts in the world. This Element discusses the nature of divine action, with a specific focus on miracles or "special" divine acts. Miracles are sometimes considered problematic. Some argue that they are theologically untenable or that they violate the laws of nature. Others claim that even if miracles occur, it is never rational to believe in them based on testimony. Still others maintain that miracles are not within the scope of historical investigation. After addressing these objections, the author examines the function of miracles as "signs" in the New Testament.

Keywords: Divine Action, Miracles, Laws of Nature, David Hume, Causation

ISBNs: 9781009475853 (HB), 9781009270335 (PB), 9781009270328 (OC)
ISSNs: 2754-8724 (online), 2754-8716 (print)

Contents

1 Miracles As Special Divine Actions

Hitler's forces, including legions of soldiers, panzers, and notorious combat planes known as the Luftwaffe, closed in upon the retreating Allied forces. The situation was dire. More than 300,000 French, Belgian, and Dutch troops were trapped on the beaches of Dunkirk, with no hope of survival unless an evacuation team could transport them across the raging waters of the English Channel. British military experts gave a grim projection, estimating that only 25 percent of the stranded soldiers would survive the Nazi onslaught. King George VI declared a national day of prayer on May 26, 1940. As the massive evacuation began, a series of fortuitous events favored the Allies. The waters of the Channel were unusually calm, allowing hundreds of small private boats to participate in the evacuation. In addition, a heavy fog and cloudy weather prevented the Luftwaffe from carrying out its dive-bombings effectively. Nearly 340,000 soldiers were evacuated to safety. This event in the early stages of World War II is commonly known as the "Dunkirk Miracle."[1]

The major monotheistic religions of the world, and indeed most human beings who have lived, believe that God has acted (and continues to act) in history. The *nature* of divine action, however, is not a simple matter. The term "divine action" can refer to a wide range of ideas, such as creation, conservation, concurrence, providence, and miracles. On the one hand, it is unsurprising that those who do not believe that God exists also deny that there are acts of God. On the other, it is striking that many *theologians* declare that miracles are impossible. According to these theologians, God neither performs miracles today nor has he done so before.

Several important questions arise in this debate: What exactly *is* a miracle? Are miracles violations of the laws of nature? What are the laws of nature in general such that they can be violated? Moreover, it seems one can be forgiven for *some* skepticism about miracles. We are all familiar with hoaxes, magic tricks, misunderstandings, and claims that eventually turn out to be spurious. But is an unqualified, universal skepticism the appropriate response to such "false positives"? Supposing that God exists, are we ever justified in thinking that a miracle has taken place? If so, what sort of evidence is required to establish its occurrence? Moreover, what is the function of miracles? What is their significance?

This Element is a philosophical and theological introduction to these topics. It consists of four sections. In Section 1, I begin by providing some terminological clarity. Although divine action encompasses a range of theologically

---

[1] For an engaging account of the Dunkirk miracle, see Lord (2017). Peterson et al. (2013: chap. 8) also open with this example.

rich concepts, the primary focus of this Element is on miracles. Miracles are commonly referred to as *special divine acts*, which I distinguish from the other related concepts. In the remainder of Section 1, I respond to several common theological arguments against the possibility of miracles.

Section 2 discusses scientific and metaphysical objections to miracles. Some maintain, for instance, that miracles would violate well-established scientific principles such as the conservation of energy or the causal closure of the physical. Others raise a more general complaint: miracles would violate the laws of nature. This point takes us into deeper philosophical terrain and raises the question of what the "laws of nature" are in the first place. Should special divine actions be characterized this way? For instance, according to some metaphysical models, the laws of nature are simply descriptions of the capacities and powers of entities in the universe. On these views, the laws of nature do not "govern" anything, and therefore miracles would not violate such laws.

In Section 3, I discuss epistemological objections to miracles, with a focus on David Hume's influential argument that belief in miracles can never be rationally justified through testimony. I maintain that several core features of Hume's argument are problematic and that a closer analysis of his argument through the lens of Bayesian probability theory reveals the weaknesses in his position.

Section 4 contains two parts. In the first, I address some objections biblical historians have raised against the possibility of investigating miracles historically. In the second part, I consider a subject that is sometimes neglected in related discussions, namely the *significance* of miracles. If we suppose that God is a personal agent who sometimes acts in the world uniquely and specially, then the question arises as to *why* he does so. What is God's purpose in bringing about miracles? Here, we begin to explore the function of miracles as *signs* (in the Greek, *semeia*) – events that point to something or someone beyond themselves.

An initial disclaimer is in order. The world's great monotheistic traditions all affirm that God acts in nature. Much of what I say in this Element, therefore, is immediately applicable to Islam, Judaism, and certain varieties of Buddhism (Talim 2002; Seeskin 2011; Thomas 2011). However, my own background and research are rooted in the Christian tradition. To a certain extent, therefore, my examples and the framework of my arguments will reflect this fact. The Christian tradition involves many different important claims. But at its core, the truth or falsity of Christianity depends on an instance of special divine action, namely the resurrection of Jesus.[2] For that

---

[2] According to 1 Corinthians 15:17, "If Christ has not been raised, your faith is futile and you are still in your sins." I will use the New Revised Standard Version unless noted otherwise.

reason, special divine action is a topic of utmost importance to the Christian: an entire worldview hinges upon it.

1.1 Initial Distinctions

Because "divine action" encompasses a range of meanings, it is important to make some distinctions in the interest of clarity. These distinctions will prepare us to address theological objections to miracles later.

1.1.1 Creation

A common conviction among monotheistic religions is that God is the creator of all things besides himself. As such, there is a clear ontological dividing line between God and everything else that exists (Bauckham 2008). Most theists have understood God's creation to be a free act: he could have refrained from creating in the first place. Had he so chosen, nothing but God would exist. Moreover, creation has typically been understood as God's bringing about the universe out of nothing (*ex nihilo*). It is not, as some of the ancient Greeks believed, that God used prior "stuff" to make the world. Instead, matter, energy, time, and space themselves appeared by God's will alone. John 1:3a puts it this way: "All things came into being through him, and without him not one thing came into being."

Throughout history, many philosophers and scientists, influenced by Greek thought, believed that the universe was eternal, without beginning or end. However, in a radical ideological shift, astrophysical discoveries over the past century have uncovered impressive evidence that the universe most likely had a beginning around 13.7 billion years ago. For some, the beginning of the universe points to God's first great act (Craig and Sinclair 2009). The beginning of the universe *ex nihilo* is one direct way of understanding God's role as creator of the cosmos.

1.1.2 Conservation

Another concept related to divine action is *conservation*. Theists have often affirmed that in addition to creating the world, God also conserves or sustains it in existence at every point in time. Without God's conserving activity moment by moment, the universe would simply cease to exist. As an illustration, consider a billiard table: the activity of the billiard balls – their rolling, colliding with each other, bouncing off edges – takes place on the surface of the table. None of these activities, however, would be possible without the table itself. The table "conserves" or "sustains" the game in existence moment by moment.

If the billiard table were suddenly to disappear, the game would be over. Similarly, God conserves the world throughout its existence, and without this sustaining activity, it would cease to be.

Some philosophers and theologians have thought that creation and conservation amount to the same thing (e.g., Quinn 1988; Suárez 2002). One way to understand this is to imagine a flip-book that produces an animation when someone quickly shuffles through the pages. The author draws a picture on each page, giving the image an appearance of continued identity. One could say that the author "conserves" the animation in being and that this conservation involves nothing more than the author's "creating" each page. Similarly, one might think that God's act of conserving the world in existence does not differ in kind from his creative work. It is beyond the scope of this project to adjudicate between these understandings of conservation.[3] For the purposes of this Element, however, I will assume that God's initial creative act and his subsequent conservation of the world are two different categories of divine activity.

1.1.3 Concurrence

The concept of *concurrence* becomes relevant when thinking about the causal role of created entities. Some thinkers, especially during the Middle Ages, grappled with the following problem. On the one hand, they wished to affirm that God is the ultimate cause of everything that happens in the universe. On the other, they maintained that creatures have their own causal powers – their own abilities to act. How can both be true? One prominent answer was that God "concurs" with creaturely causes. That is to say: God and creatures bring about effects together but in different ways. The tricky part is specifying what these "different ways" are. Thomas Aquinas thought that one could understand the relationship between divine and creaturely activity in terms of primary and secondary causation.[4] To borrow an example from Ignacio Silva (2022: 99–100), imagine someone who is cutting a piece of bread with a knife. The knife has its own causal powers by virtue of its slender shape, hardness, sharp edge, and so forth. When someone cuts the bread, the knife is therefore a cause, but it

---

[3] For a discussion, see Vander Laan (2022).

[4] We should note, however, that Aquinas himself distinguishes between God's general concurrence and special divine acts (miracles), such as those described in Scripture (Silva 2022: 102–5). He writes that

> divine power can sometimes produce an effect … apart from the order implanted in natural things by God. In fact, he does this at times to manifest his power. For it can be manifested in no better way … than by the fact that sometimes he does something outside the order of nature. Indeed, this makes it evident that the order of things has proceeded from him, not by natural necessity, but by free will (1956: 79).

is only a secondary cause. The primary cause is the person who uses the knife as an instrument. Similarly, God is the primary cause who works through all the secondary causes we find in nature.

Concurrentists are drawn to this picture because it preserves God's causal role in everything that occurs. They see concurrentism as a middle position between two objectionable views, *occasionalism* and *mere conservationism*. According to occasionalism, there is no causation between natural entities. Instead, every apparent instance of causation is, in fact, divine causation. When two billiard balls collide, it may appear that one is setting the other into motion. But in reality, when the billiard balls meet, this is an "occasion" when God acts: he causes the first ball to stop and then sends the next ball on its trajectory. Some philosophers during the modern period, most notably Nicholas Malebranche, accepted varieties of this view. From the concurrentists' perspective, occasionalism is unacceptable because it prioritizes God's causal role to the exclusion of creaturely causation.

Mere conservationism is the position that God's activity (setting aside miracles for the moment) is restricted to his initial act of creation and his subsequent conservation of the universe. On this view, God allows natural entities and their own causal powers to "play out" throughout time. Of course, mere conservationists may affirm that God performs miracles throughout history (for that reason, mere conservationism does not imply deism since deists additionally reject miracles). Concurrentists, however, find mere conservationism objectionable on the basis that it detracts from God's role as primary cause.

The viability of the concurrentist position depends on how one thinks that primary and secondary causation work together. Some philosophers and theologians argue that concurrentism ultimately leads to untenable consequences (Frost 2014; Kittle 2022).[5] That debate, however, falls beyond the scope of this Element. For now, we will proceed on the assumption that God and creatures are related as primary and secondary causes, even if we cannot settle on the exact nature of this relationship here.

1.1.4 Special Divine Action

The final category, the one that will occupy us throughout the rest of the Element, is that of special divine actions, which I will use interchangeably

---

[5] In my view, the challenges to concurrentism are important. For instance, humans often cause evil actions, which seems to imply that God, as the primary cause, is also responsible for evil. Moreover, it is unclear whether concurrentism is necessary in addition to other types of divine action. Plantinga (2008: 396n2) describes the suspicion of Peter van Inwagen that concurrence "is no more than a matter of paying God superfluous metaphysical complements; why add this to all the rest?"

with the term "miracles." The qualification "special" is meant, somewhat artificially, to distinguish such events from "general" divine actions. Now that we've discussed creation, conservation, and concurrence (the three Cs), we can think of these as falling under the category of God's general acts. Special divine actions, by contrast, are those acts of God beyond his creation of the world, his conserving it in being, and his concurring with natural causes.

To approach it differently, we might think of some paradigmatic instances of special divine actions: the parting of the Red Sea, water turning into wine, instantaneous restorations of sight, and Jesus' resurrection from the dead. These are events that most plausibly go beyond the domain of the three Cs. They are cases in which God goes "above and beyond" his usual activity in the world and does something new for specific reasons and in specific circumstances. For now, this will provide us with a working description of special divine actions.

1.1.5 Providence

The idea of *providence* is conceptually separate from special divine actions, though the two are related (Luck 2016: 274–5). Providence is a broader notion having to do with God's benevolent guidance, control, and plan for the world. Debates about divine providence typically center around the *mechanism* of God's sovereign influence: Does God bring about his benefi-cent ends by determining everything that occurs throughout history? Or does he allow "room" in the unfolding universe for various events – for instance, the free responses of humans? Providence can also simply refer to God's act of taking care of people as parents take care of their children. It is evident that special divine acts may fit into a broader understanding of providence. God may, for instance, bring about his purposes in history by virtue of performing miracles. Nevertheless, providence and special divine acts are two conceptually distinct ideas, and my discussion will focus on the latter.

1.2 Theological Arguments against Miracles

We may now proceed to ask more substantial questions about miracles them-selves. A surprising number of theologians, often working from assumptions born in the Enlightenment, deny that special divine acts are possible. Such theologians typically acknowledge God's role as creator and sustainer of the universe, but for various reasons regard as unpalatable the idea that God would act *specially* – in a manner that goes against the usual, regular course of nature. In this section, I will examine and respond to five such arguments.

1.2.1 The Argument from Self-Contradiction

According to one line of thought, God doesn't perform miracles because doing so would involve God's working against himself or his own activity. He would be engaged in a type of self-undermining behavior. The influential theologian Paul Tillich, for instance, asserts, "Miracles cannot be interpreted in terms of supranatural interference in natural processes. If such an interpretation were true, the manifestation of the ground of being would destroy the structure of being; God would be split within himself" (1953: 129).

Tillich, in typical enigmatic fashion, seems to object to the idea of an "interference" in the natural world. In Section 2, I will discuss whether this term reflects the appropriate language to use for special divine acts. But let that pass for now. What might we say about Tillich's claim that "the manifestation of the ground of being would destroy the structure of being"? It's difficult to know exactly what Tillich means here. But if we frame the objection in terms of the distinctions we made earlier, Tillich seems to be suggesting that God's activity as creator and sustainer of the universe (i.e., God as the ground of being) implies that no more divine activity is needed or allowed. If God were to cause miracles, this would disrupt the "structure of being" that has been established by his creative and sustaining roles. In that sense, God would be "split."

The same reasoning also appears in the literature of the eighteenth-century deists (though Tillich would resist such a label himself). Thomas Morgan, for example, explains that God never suspends or alters the laws of nature because "[s]uch a supposition would be unworthy of God, as the creator and governor of the world, and the universal cause, preserver, and director of nature" (1741: 76).

This argument (if it is an argument) has little to commend it. Why believe that once a particular "structure" has been set in place – once God has created and continues to sustain the universe – God cannot act in ways that go beyond that structure (Larmer 2013: 116)? Perhaps Tillich thinks that God imposes a kind of self-limitation by virtue of causing and sustaining the universe. If so, then we would need an additional argument for that conclusion. Moreover, it is far from clear why divine activity beyond creation and conservation would be "unworthy of God" as Morgan suggests. Does "unworthy" in this context mean inconsistent? Where is the inconsistency? Does it simply mean undignified or beneath God? If so, then once again, this assertion needs to be supported.

Indeed, it's somewhat easy to imagine why special divine actions might in fact be worthy of God. If God's universe contains free, rational agents capable of relating to and interacting with God himself, then he might occasionally choose to intervene in the natural world in order to reveal himself, answer prayers, or directly relate to humans. Perhaps God is, as Benedikt Göcke puts it, "like a piano player whose left hand constantly plays the same chord," and miracles "can be seen as his right hand adding now and then some fine tunes in order to create the overall melody of creation" (2015: 26). So, without further support this objection remains unpersuasive.

1.2.2 The Argument from Transcendence

Another argument against miracles is that they would compromise divine transcendence. Part of the difficulty in assessing this argument is that the term "transcendence" is multivalent and all theists will accept at least some meaning of it. For example, theists acknowledge that God is far above us, infinite in knowledge, power, perfect in moral status, and so on. Similarly, one might understand transcendence as referring to God's unique causal roles, such as being the creator and sustainer of the world who also concurs with creatures' actions. If so, then the response to the previous argument also applies in this case: there is no reason to believe that God cannot act beyond his creative, conserving, and concurring roles.

Many philosophers and theologians, however, have interpreted God's transcendence in a much stronger sense. On this view, God is so far beyond us – so wholly other – that he is utterly unknowable, incomprehensible, and ineffable. Some suggest that this strong understanding of transcendence also creates problems for special divine acts. Denis Edwards, for instance, claims that God cannot be a "cause among other causes" because that would go against "the absolute mystery and transcendence of the Creator" (2010: 63). He continues:

> The incomprehensible God is, by definition, the one beyond our knowing. Whatever we can comprehend is not God, but a construct of our minds . . . We never find any particular point of intersection (the "causal joint") between God and creatures, because we have no empirical access to God. . . . So a theology of divine action not only should not spell out how God acts, but should insist that this is something we cannot know. (63)

The justification for Edwards's agnosticism about the nature of divine action is highly suspect. The fact that no one has "empirical access" to God is inconsequential because it is false that one must have empirical access to something as a prerequisite for knowing about it. Here we might think about abstract objects such as numbers, sets, and propositions – entities to which we have no empirical access but about which we know a great deal. Moreover, if special divine acts do occur, then they are arguably the "points of intersection" or "causal joints" that Edwards claims we do not have.

Furthermore, it is difficult to avoid the conclusion that Edwards's own position is self-undermining. In the end, he appeals to a version of concurrentism – that God acts as primary cause through natural secondary causes – as his preferred model of divine action.[6] But if God is truly unknowable, so far beyond us such that our language can never capture any truth about him, then the same is also true of statements about God's transcendence – that he is the primary cause of all things, that miracles take place exclusively through secondary causes, and so on. Edwards is surprisingly candid about this latter point. He writes, "There is a great deal that can be said about special divine acts, and I am trying to say some important things about them ... But it is inappropriate to think we can describe the nature of divine action, because to do so would be to describe the nature of God" (2010: 64). Again, it is hard to avoid the appearance of self-contradiction: Edwards denies our ability to describe the nature of divine action and then proceeds to describe it. So it seems to me that appealing to indissoluble mystery as the ground for complete agnosticism about divine action is ultimately wrongheaded. Such a position implies that we are unable to affirm propositions about God that all theists do (or should) affirm – for instance, that he providentially guides the world, that he loves his creatures, and that he intends the best for them (Kittle 2022: 251–6).

1.2.3 The Argument from Free Will

Another line of reasoning against miracles is that they would undermine the possibility of autonomous creatures with free will. George Ellis, for instance, claims:

> [I]t seems probable that fixed laws of behavior of matter, independent of interference by a Creator ... is a requisite basis of existence of independent beings able to exercise free will, for they make possible meaningful complex organized activity without outside interference (physical laws providing a determinate frame within which definite local causal relations are possible). Thus we envisage the creator choosing such a framework for the universe (thus giving up all other possibilities allowed by the power available to him, such as the power to directly intervene in events by overruling the laws of physics from time to time). (Ellis 1999: 384)

Here Ellis thinks of a "determinate frame" that he envisions as organized complex activity behaving regularly and predictably. So the argument is that this determinate frame, which is established by the laws of nature, is a necessary condition for creatures to have free will. If God were to intervene in the world,

---

[6] Edwards attributes this view to Aquinas. We have already seen, however, that Aquinas allows for divine intervention beyond secondary causation. See footnote 4.

he would undermine the laws of nature within this determinate frame. And this, in turn, would undermine free will.

This argument, however, is problematic. In Section 2, I will argue that it is not necessary to think that miracles violate the laws of nature, especially if such laws are understood only as formalized descriptions of the causal powers in the world. So, once again, language about "interfering with" with the laws is dispensable. However, Ellis's main concern seems to be about regularity or predictability. The idea is that there must be some sort of regular, predictable framework in order for free creatures to act in meaningful ways. How so?

Suppose I am driving my car to the supermarket when I receive word that some friends are meeting up at a local restaurant. I have the ability to choose whether to continue driving to the supermarket or to divert my course to meet up with them. However, special divine acts could undermine my free will if God, for example, were to interfere with my immediate environment by randomly causing gravity to cease operating, suddenly rearranging the roads in front of me, or causing me to forget directions. These scenarios seem to be the kind of freedom-undermining situations that concern Ellis.

The unwarranted assumption, however, is that God's intervening in the world *must* generate the sort of disruption that would undermine free will. But why believe that? If one thinks that God has performed miracles in the past – healing the blind, parting the Red Sea, or raising Jesus from the dead – how do *those* miracles undermine my free decisions right now? Obviously, they don't. All one needs to suppose is that special divine actions happen occasionally, but not in a way that would undermine the regularity/predictability associated with free actions generally. As Alvin Plantinga puts it: "All that's required for free action is reasonable confidence in the substantial regularity in the neighborhood of the proposed action. And that's certainly compatible with God's sometimes intervening" (2008: 386).

1.2.4 The Argument from Coercion

Another related argument against miracles is that they would involve "divine coercion." According to Thomas Oord, the regularities found in nature are a product of God's all-loving nature, which is fundamentally incompatible with coercive acts. Oord's view of divine coercion refers to unilateral divine activity that occurs without any consent or cooperation from creatures, whether human or nonhuman. As a consequence, God cannot and does not interfere with lawlike regularities (Oord 2015: 175). "If God can control creatures or interrupt creation's consistencies by absolute fiat, God can coerce" (191).

Now, somewhat surprisingly, Oord affirms that miracles do in fact occur, but he attempts to explain them, especially biblical miracles, in terms of *non*coercive divine influence. He writes,

> Miracles occur when creatures, organisms or entities of various size and complexity cooperate with God's initiating and empowering love … I know of no miracles described in the Bible or that believers have witnessed in history that require God to coerce … No biblical text explicitly supports divine coercion, including those texts addressing the initial creation of the world, the incarnation of Jesus, God's resurrecting Jesus from the dead, the ultimate destiny of creation (eschaton) and all events between. (2015: 200–1)

Again, when Oord speaks of coercion, he is referring to unilateral divine activity without creaturely consent or cooperation. When Jesus heals people, he does so with their cooperation (e.g., the blind request to regain their sight). Thus, such miracles do not count as coercive.

There are two major problems, it seems to me, with this view. The first is that it's unclear why instances of divine intervention must count as "coercive" when free creatures are not involved (Larmer 2021: 191). The terms "coercion" and "cooperation" do not appear to be applicable to things such as rocks, stars, weather, wine, and water. Coercion carries moral connotations, and it seems simply confused to say that when God prevents a boulder from falling off a cliff, this is an instance of divine *coercion* against the boulder. Without these moral connotations, however, it is doubtful that such divine interventions contradict the view that God is all-loving. Perhaps we might understand "cooperation" in terms of God's concurrence with natural powers. But as we saw earlier, this need not exclude divine activity beyond concurrence.

My second objection is that biblical miracles seem squarely at odds with Oord's position. On his view, lawlike regularities are a direct consequence of the nature of divine love, which implies natural regularities cannot be broken. Yet Oord is open to biblical miracles as long as they are interpreted in a noncoercive manner. The problem is that such miracles – even if they are brought about cooperatively – themselves cause a break in nature's regularities. We only need to think of the healing of the blind, instant remissions of leprosy, the feeding of multitudes with two loaves and five fish, exorcisms, and the resurrections of Jairus's daughter, Lazarus, and, ultimately, Jesus. Such miracles clearly defy the regularities found in nature, even if they are done with the recipients' cooperation.[7]

---

[7] Elsewhere, Oord attempts to account for the resurrection of Jesus in noncoercive terms (2010: 150–2). But his explanation, which appeals to the yet-responsive stimuli in Jesus' dead body and Jesus' "cooperating" with God through his divine nature while physically dead, is, to put it bluntly, bizarre.

Problems become even more acute for this view when one considers nature miracles (i.e., those not involving free creatures). Consider the parting of the Red Sea. On a straightforward understanding of the story, God controls the waters and pushes them back by means of a great wind. Oord rejects this view. His first complaint is that special divine activity thus understood raises the problem of "selective miracles," namely that if God were capable of intervening occasionally, he would intervene more often (or all the time) in order to prevent evil. Oord writes,

> Explanations of the Red Sea miracle relying upon divine control arise from the implicit view that God's power logically precedes divine love. This view raises the problem of selective miracles ... Why didn't the God capable of the supernatural control of inanimate objects prevent the detonation of the bombs at the Boston Marathon? ... Why doesn't God use supernatural control to prevent a host of genuine evils ... ? (2015: 208)

I will address the argument of "selective miracles" later in this Element. For now, however, it is quite strange that Oord advances this as an objection to divine intervention. For he then immediately attempts to explain how God might bring about the parting of the Red Sea in noncoercive manner. He envisions the following possibilities (2015: 209–10): (i) God may use random, spontaneous events, perhaps at the quantum level, to account for the parting of the Red Sea. (ii) The actions of free creatures (Moses, the Israelites, Pharaoh's army, etc.) might have been the catalysts of a great natural chain reaction that resulted in the parting of the Red Sea. (iii) God may have predicted the weather patterns and known that there was a high likelihood that the waters would part/ dry up; he then instructed Moses through a "still small voice" to guide the Israelites through at the right time.

One will note right away that strategies (i) and (iii) are of no help to Oord because they confront his own problem of selective miracles: if God used random, spontaneous events at the Red Sea, why doesn't he do so to prevent other instances of evil? If God instructed Moses through a "still small voice," then why didn't he do something similar in the case of the Boston Marathon bombings or 9/11 or the Holocaust? Strategy (ii) strikes me as supremely, irredeemably odd. Is the idea *really* that the actions of human beings – for example, the pattering of Israelite sandals on the desert sand miles away – naturally brought about the parting of the Red Sea? Such a view strains credulity.

In sum, the argument that divine interventions are impossible because they would amount to divine coercion is unpersuasive. It's unclear how divine love entails the existence of unbreakable lawlike regularities. Moreover, this picture becomes increasingly implausible if one also believes in the possibility of biblical miracles, which, to all appearances, do involve divine intervention.

1.2.5 The Argument from Evil

Perhaps the most popular argument against the possibility of special divine acts comes from the existence of preventable evils. We have already seen Oord's objection that divine interventions raise the further question of why God doesn't intervene in other circumstances in order to prevent evil. In the same vein, Christine Overall declares, "When alleged miracles purport to make a major change (as in raising Lazarus from the dead), they solve the problems of only a select few, ignoring almost all of the unmet needs, deliberate cruelty, and enormous suffering in both human and non-human beings" (2014: 608). Similarly, Ellis claims, "[T]he question arises as to why [miraculous intervention] happens so seldom. If this is allowed at all to achieve some good, why is it not allowed all the time, to assuage my toothache as well as the evils of Auschwitz?" (2000: 383).

In response, we should first recognize that the objection is an instance or subcategory of the broader question of why God allows evil in general. Given the vast literature on the problem of evil and its sundry formulations and rejoinders, a full treatment goes beyond the scope of this Element.[8]

Nevertheless, we can make a few observations regarding the argument, particularly concerning miracles. First, even if one cannot *identify* why God refrains from performing a miracle, it does not follow that God cannot or does not have such a reason. This is not a matter of handwaving or ignoring the problem. Rather, it is a consequence of our limited epistemic standpoint due to our spatiotemporal limitations and finite cognitive abilities. For all we know, the reason that God allows some instances of evil (by not intervening with a miracle) might be to bring about a greater good that is beyond anything we could predict, imagine, or even comprehend (Bergmann 2001).

Imagine two hungry toddlers sitting at the lunch table. Their mother "intervenes" by handing one toddler some food, but she gives nothing to the second toddler even though he is visibly hungry. The second toddler is saddened and upset: why does his mother give food to his brother but not to him? To all appearances, the mother is unfair and perhaps even unloving. What the hungry toddler does not know, however, is that later during the day he is scheduled to undergo a medical procedure that requires that he not eat anything prior to the treatment. The mother, in other words, has reasons not to give the toddler lunch

---

[8] See Plantinga (1989), Van Inwagen (2008), Stump (2012), and Peterson (2022).

that day – reasons that are beyond the capacity of the toddler to understand. Yet surely, we are often at a similar, even greater, epistemic distance from God's providential reasons. This consideration should make us skeptical of our ability to declare God's malevolence in the absence of divine intervention.

Second, even if most of the time we are unable to know why God refrains from bringing about miracles, we may nevertheless come up with some possible reasons. Note that one does not need to affirm that such reasons are God's *actual* reasons but only that they perhaps are. For instance, consider a world in which God intervenes miraculously to prevent all evils. Such a world would plausibly be at odds with the existence of morally responsible free creatures. As mentioned earlier, agents endowed with libertarian freedom may, by virtue of being free, choose to commit evil actions – on scales small and large. Miraculous divine interventions to prevent all evil actions or the consequences of such actions would in many cases undermine human autonomy and moral responsibility.

We might imagine further what a world in which God prevents every evil would look like. Suppose that God were to intervene to cure every headache, that he were to redirect all dangerous boulders falling off cliffs, that he were always to calm the waters when people are endangered by storms at sea, that he were to prevent all blindness and other illnesses. One likely consequence is that no one would be able to *identify* special divine acts as such. Divine intervention would become a regular, expected, predictable phenomenon that we would attribute to world's natural functioning. Perhaps, however, God desires to use miracles as ways of conveying a message or pointing to something beyond the natural world. In Section 4, I will discuss this point in greater detail. For now, we may note that if miracles were ubiquitous to the point where they were unrecognizable, then they could not function as signs in this way.

In sum, the present argument against miracles is a subcategory of the general problem of evil. A more nuanced answer would depend on addressing the latter. We should recognize, however, that given our epistemic limitations, it would be unwise to deny God's all-lovingness because he sometimes does not intervene when we think he ought to. Moreover, it may well be the case that a world flourishing with morally responsible, free creatures who can recognize miracles as divine signs would be impossible if God were to prevent every instance of evil.

1.3 Conclusion

This section began by analyzing various ways of understanding divine actions. Miracles, I suggested, are to be distinguished from God's initial act of creation, his subsequent conservation of the universe in existence, and his concurrence with creaturely actions. Miracles, moreover, may play a role in God's providential guidance, but the two concepts should be kept separate.

We also examined several theological objections to miracles. The arguments from self-contradiction and transcendence failed to distinguish the various modes of divine activity or offered no reasons against the possibility of special divine acts. The argument from free will mistakenly assumed miracles would disrupt all regularities needed for the activity of free creatures. The argument from coercion was problematic both in its understanding of divine love and of biblical miracles. Finally, I indicated that the argument from evil is a subcategory of the broader problem of evil. God may have reasons for not intervening to prevent evil, even if we cannot always specify with confidence what those reasons are.

2 Science, Metaphysics, and Miracles

This section examines four arguments against miracles that appeal to science or to principles that are often part of scientific discourse. The first is the so-called causal closure of the physical, which claims that the physical world is sealed off from any sort of nonphysical influence – including God's. The second is the principle of conservation of energy, which some see as a scientific problem for divine action. The third is an objection known as the "pairing problem," the claim that immaterial entities cannot be connected or paired with physical ones. Finally, I address the argument that the laws of nature cannot be violated, but that miracles would be violations of such laws. The problem with this argument is that the nature of the laws is often left unspecified. In fact, there are at least five metaphysical models of the laws of nature. I argue that the objection fails on each of them. Indeed, I suggest we should leave aside the definition of miracles as law violations, and I offer a more precise characterization in terms of causal powers.

2.1 Causal Closure of the Physical

Advocates of the causal closure of the physical affirm that physical events – planetary movements, weather patterns, brain processes – have purely physical causes. Here is one version of the principle proposed by Jaegwon Kim (2007: 15):

(K) If a physical event has a cause at t, then it has a physical cause at t.

The idea is that the universe is composed of a tightly woven causal nexus of physical events, and there is no causal influence from outside the physical realm. So, if God were to intervene in the world and produce a miracle, this would be an instance of external causation by a nonphysical entity and therefore a violation of K.[9]

The suggestion is that the physical world is causally self-contained. While entities such as God, angels, Cartesian souls, and a whole host of nonphysical entities *may* exist, these entities do not "causally meddle with physical events – that is, there can be no causal influences injected into the physical domain from outside" (Kim 2007: 16).

The same idea is sometimes expressed in terms of the "completeness of physics." Physical completeness, according to David Papineau (2007: 8), rests on the following principle:

(P) All physical effects are fully determined by law by prior physical occurrences.

The term "determined" also covers probabilistic occurrences such as might be found at the quantum level. If there are physical events that are brought about probabilistically, then their chances are determined by the prior physical states (Papineau 2007: 33n2). Again, we are left with no room for nonphysical causal intervention (whether mental or divine).

The question we must ask is: Why think that K and P are true? What justification might be offered in their favor? Surprisingly, for as much attention as such principles receive, it's difficult to advance any compelling argument on their behalf. First, theists will (or should) immediately reject K and P because they imply that God did not create the world. The first moment of creation was a physical event that had neither a physical cause (God is nonphysical) nor any prior physical occurrences (since it was the first moment). So, while atheists, who don't believe in divine intervention anyway, might accept K and P, theists should not.

Second, we should recognize that K and P are not mathematical or logical truths; their negations don't imply contradictions. Nor are they definitional truths such as, for example, that all bachelors are unmarried males. So why think K and P are true? It is implausible that they could be established a priori. Recognizing this, Papineau attempts to formulate an empirical or inductive argument on behalf the completeness of physics (2007). At its core, his argument is that if nonphysical (mental) causation indeed takes place in the physical world, we should be able to detect it empirically – for example, by pointing to instances of anomalous acceleration (30). Yet no evidence of this kind has been

---

[9] Strictly speaking, in order to exclude special divine acts, K needs to be supplemented by a non-overdetermination principle (which Kim later provides [2007: 17]). The idea is that physical events have exclusively physical causes. For various formulations and critiques of causal closure principles, see Montero (2003) and Lowe (2008: 41–57).

forthcoming, at least not in the past seven decades of research. So, this provides inductive support for the completeness of physics.

In the context of the philosophy of mind, one common rejoinder to the "lack of evidence" argument is to challenge the assumption that nonphysical causation would be detectable in the way Papineau and others anticipate. E. J. Lowe, for instance, argues that mental causation, while still making a difference in the world, may be "invisible" to empirical investigation. The reason is that mental states may only serve to render physical processes non-coincidental (2008: 27–40, 74–8). If Lowe is correct, then nonphysical influence does not work through "pushes" or "pulls" or "anomalous accelerations." So, Papineau's inductive argument against nonphysical causation would be a nonstarter.

More importantly, however, we should note that scientific investigation into nonphysical causes takes a different shape outside the philosophy of mind context. Part of the assumption (a reasonable one) in the philosophy of mind literature is that *if* mental causation occurs, it takes place regularly, predictably, and within the person's body/brain. We all have beliefs, desires, and other mental states that, by hypothesis, cause physical behavior. In this context, scientific investigation is in principle more straightforward since we can isolate the "arena" in which nonphysical causation is supposed to take place (you can attach electrodes to my head and examine electrical activity, etc.). But the case of special divine intervention is different. If miracles are acts of a supernatural agent who is free to intervene whenever and wherever he wills, then we have reason to suppose that miracles might be irregular, sometimes unpredictable, and not always in isolated places where scientific inquiry could gather the data needed to support (or disconfirm) K and P. Perhaps God will choose to heal someone on the plains of the Serengeti today but not tomorrow. Perhaps he chose to change water into wine at a wedding party in first-century Cana but not at wedding reception in twenty-first-century St. Louis. If this is right, it casts serious doubt on any inductive argument for the conclusion that the world is causally closed or that physics is complete in a way that miracles are excluded.

2.2 Conservation of Energy

A related objection to miracles has to do with the principle of conservation of energy (PCE) – a veritable pillar in the science of thermodynamics. What is PCE? The following description comes from a recent authoritative physics textbook:

> [I]n any physical system free from outside influences, *energy* does not change with time. This fact is referred to as conservation of energy, and this is energy's most fundamental attribute. In fact, energy is important in science

precisely because it is conserved. While it moves easily and often from one system to another and changes form in ways that are sometimes difficult to follow, energy can neither be created nor destroyed. It is possible to understand the behavior of most physical systems by following the flow of energy through them. (Jaffe and Taylor 2018: 3, italics in original)

In other words, PCE says that in closed systems (those free of outside influences), the amount of energy in that system may change forms but is always constant. It is pivotal to recognize that the principle contains the qualifiers, "closed," "isolated," and "free from outside influences" (Jaffe and Taylor 2018: 404–5). If that condition is not met, then energy may not be conserved within the system after all.

Unfortunately, those who wish to exclude special divine acts often misunderstand PCE. For instance, William Stoeger objects to miracles because they "would involve an immaterial agent acting on or within a material context ... This is not possible; if it were, either energy and information would be added to a system spontaneously and mysteriously contravening the conservation of energy" (2009: 118).

Contrary to Stoeger, if God were to bring new energy into a physical system (say, the system that includes the Red Sea), then that system would fail to be closed (Plantinga 2008: 374–5). As a result, there would be no contravention or violation of PCE. Objections such as Stoeger's may give the impression that there are "pockets" of closed systems throughout nature. In reality, however, all physical systems in the universe are influenced by surrounding systems. Thus, PCE functions similarly to ideal gas laws: they are useful and express genuine physical truths, even though no actual system behaves exactly as they describe (Larmer 2014: 44).

It might be suggested that the universe as a whole is a closed system, but such a claim would venture into metaphysical territory beyond the scope of PCE (Plantinga 2011: 78–9). Merely asserting that the universe is closed would beg the question against the theist, since if God were to intervene by adding or subtracting energy from the universe, then the universe would not be a closed system after all.

Now, PCE is sometimes (mistakenly) used interchangeably with the proposition:

(NC) Energy can neither be created nor destroyed.

Many physicists, including Robert Jaffe and Washington Taylor, sometimes use such language. But equating PCE with NC fails to capture what scientists mean. The point is that when energy is transferred from one system to another, *it may change forms*: chemical energy (food) may transform into kinetic energy (bodily motion); electrical energy (in an outlet) may be converted into heat (in a toaster); energy from light may transform into chemical energy (in plants). Yet throughout such processes, no new energy "pops into being" or vanishes from existence. This is what statements like NC are supposed to convey. They are emphatically *not* supposed to be some metaphysical principle that would proscribe divine intervention. Not only would such a claim venture beyond what science can establish, it would also imply that God could not have created the world.

In other words, a theist who believes in miracles may wholeheartedly agree with PCE but should also affirm that any system in which God intervenes is not a closed, isolated system. J. L. Mackie, not a theist himself, captures the idea correctly: we must "regard the whole natural world as being, for most of the time, such a closed system; we can then think of a supernatural intervention as something that intrudes into that system from outside the natural world as a whole" (1983: 21).[10]

Divine intervention is therefore compatible with PCE. Some may still argue, however, that we have never detected any influxes of energy that we could not account for, and this suggests inductively that miracles do not take place. Evan Fales claims, for instance:

> I suggest that we have evidence – abundant evidence – that the only sources of energy are natural ones. Our evidence is just this: whenever we are able to balance the books on the energy (and momentum) of a physical system, and find an increase or decrease, and we look hard enough for a physical explanation of that increase or decrease, we find one. There is no case in which, given sufficient understanding of the system, we have failed to find such a physical explanation. (2010: 16)

This objection is similar to the one we saw earlier. Fales avers that if miracles occur, they introduce new energy into the universe – specifically, into whatever physical system God acts within at that time. So, when God intervenes to divide the Red Sea, new energy is introduced then and there. The objection, however, is that we have observed plenty of physical systems, and in no case have we needed to postulate a new, unaccountable source of energy.

Fales's argument, however, is problematic. Part of my earlier reply to Papineau applies here as well: the argument assumes that divine interventions must take place in controlled, isolated contexts where unaccounted energy might be detected. But, of course, none of this is guaranteed if special divine actions are the products of a free agent who is under no obligation to act in a way

---

[10] The term "intrusion" carries some negative connotations that are unnecessary to Mackie's point (but we may give him a pass since he gets the rest right).

that allows us to "balance the books on the energy." So, a key assumption of the argument is false.

Now, perhaps we should interpret Fales to mean that we never find anomalous influxes of energy in a general sense (not necessarily in a scientifically isolated context). In other words, we don't see instant healings or great partings of water or resurrections. Interpreted this way, however, the argument boils down to the highly unimpressive claim that miracles don't happen because we've never witnessed any (an argument that will receive our attention in Section 3). But the conservation-of-energy principle – that which coated the argument with a scientific veneer – no longer plays a central role in the argument. So, in the end, Fales's line of reasoning either rests on a false assumption about the nature of special divine acts or else it is reducible to a weak and uninspiring (and nonscientific) argument.

2.3 Causal Pairing

Another argument against special divine actions comes from further considerations in the philosophy of mind. Many philosophers throughout history have thought that there are two dimensions or aspects associated with human beings: a physical aspect (the body) and a nonphysical aspect (the soul). One version of this position, known as *substance dualism*, affirms that a person is identical to her soul but that she is causally related or connected to a material body. Varieties of this view can be found most famously in the writings of Plato and René Descartes. While substance dualism is not the majority position today, it has no paucity of defenders.[11]

One of the most prominent arguments against substance dualism is to question the very intelligibility of causation between immaterial and material entities. If successful, the argument would have implications for special divine acts as well. Kim, for example, gives the following example involving causation between physical objects:

> [T]wo guns, A and B, are simultaneously fired, and this results in the simultaneous death of two persons, Adam and Bob. What makes it the case that the firing of A caused Adam's death and the firing of B caused Bob's death, and not the other way around? What are the principles that underlie the correct and incorrect pairings of cause and effect in a situation like this? We call this the "causal pairing problem." (2007: 78–9)

Kim asks: Why is one gun "paired" with one person instead of another? Why does A kill Adam and not Bob? The straightforward answer, of course, is that

---

[11] For an informative exposition of the different varieties and defenses of substance dualism, see Menuge et al. (2018).

A is *pointed* at Adam, and B is pointed at Bob. The guns are spatially oriented in such a way that they are paired with their targets. So, what are the pairing relations in Kim's example? The answer: *spatial relations*.

But now consider a parallel thought experiment involving souls. On substance dualism, souls are causally connected to bodies. Suppose that two souls, A and B, simultaneously perform an identical mental action, and as a result a change occurs in the physical world – say, your hand goes up. Suppose further that soul A, not soul B, in fact caused this physical change. The question is: *Why* is it that soul A caused your hand to go up, but soul B did not? What are the pairing relations between souls and physical things? Notice that in this case we can't appeal to spatial relations because souls are, by hypothesis, nonspatial.[12] Souls aren't "pointed at" anything. So, substance dualism is in trouble because there is no plausible way of causally connecting souls with bodies.[13]

Now, the reason for articulating the causal pairing problem against substance dualism here is that a parallel argument can be lodged against special divine actions. There is an interesting conceptual connection between how dualists think a person is causally related to her body and how theists believe God is causally related to the universe. After all, God is an immaterial, nonspatial mind who, on the traditional view, has a certain control over the material world in a direct way. The parallel objection, in other words, is that there are no spatial relations between God and the universe that might serve to "pair" the two. So, God does not causally interact with the world.[14]

More precisely, the argument seems to be:

(1) If two things interact causally, there is a pairing relation between them.

(2) Pairing relations obtain only between spatial things.

(3) God is nonspatial.

Therefore,

(4) God doesn't causally interact with anything.

Now premise (3) will be accepted by most theists. Although God's omnipresence is a pillar of orthodox theology, it has not traditionally been understood in a spatial manner.[15] The challenging premises are therefore (1) and (2).

---

[12] Some dualists think the soul is spatially extended: see Hasker (1999: 192). Eleonore Stump (1995; 2003: 200–3), following Aquinas, understands the soul (the "form" of the body) as spatially extended.

[13] For a response to Kim's argument, see Bailey et al. (2011).

[14] Evan Fales (2010) articulates a pairing problem against special divine action. See Ganssle (2021) for a direct response.

[15] Though see Buckareff (2016) for an alternative view.

As a preliminary response, we should immediately notice that those who accept the conjunction of (1) and (2) must deny that God created the world. The reason is that creation involves causation (Bailey et al. 2011: 351). Since the creation of the world is an essential tenet of theism, no theist will be persuaded by the present argument. But we may still go further, for there are reasons to doubt both (1) and (2). The first premise again states:

(1) If two things interact causally, there is a pairing relation between them.

The idea is that for causation to obtain between x and y, there must be some property of x or y or some other (noncausal) relation that "connects" the two. But why believe this? Some philosophers reject this requirement outright and defend a view known as "singularism" about causation according to which causality is a basic relation and independent of the (nontrivial) properties of x and y (e.g., Tooley 1997: 93–101; Audi 2011). Applied to our current discussion, this position would imply that no prerequisite pairing relation is necessary between God and, say, the Red Sea for God to act upon it. That God is causally related to the various entities in the world is a brute fact requiring no explanation in terms of some other pairing features.

Let us grant, however, for the sake of argument, that pairing relations are required for causal relations to obtain. The second premise is even more problematic:

(2) Pairing relations obtain only between spatial things.

Is it true that pairing relations are necessarily spatial? If we reason inductively based on the causal relations we observe in the physical world, we might be inclined to think so. However, this inductive strategy is limited to things in space and time – the domain of empirical investigation. Therefore, such an inductive argument for (2) would be inadequate, since (2) is a claim about *all* pairing relations, even those outside the scope of empirical inquiry.

In fact, we may go beyond simply demonstrating the lack of support for (2). Some philosophers point to *intentionality* as a mental feature that functions as a pairing link between a soul/mind and its object (e.g., Ganssle 2021). A thing has the property of intentionality when it is *about something else*. For instance, I am now thinking about the Taj Mahal; the Taj Mahal is the content of my current mental state. In other words, there is a mental connection or pairing between me and something else, but this pairing is nonspatial. It's not that my thought is "pointed at" the Taj Mahal in the way that gun A was pointed at Adam. Instead, it's that the Taj Majal is what my thought is *about*. Furthermore, this intentional feature of the mind allows me to make decisions and interact causally with the world – for example, I plan our next family vacation to see the Taj Mahal instead of going elsewhere.

The nature of intentionality, in addition to some classical divine properties, may provide insight into how God is "paired" with the spatial, material world. According to classical theism, God is omniscient, which means he knows all truths and believes no falsehoods. This implies that God has thoughts about every single spatial/material entity because he knows true propositions about them. Some have argued that God also has direct, nonpropositional knowledge of everything in the universe (Alston 1986). On this latter view, every material entity is immediately "present" to God in the same way that qualitative states (e.g., being in pain) are immediately present to us. Either way, divine intentionality serves as the pairing relation demanded by Kim and others, even if that pairing relation is not spatial (Ganssle 2021: 278–81).

In sum, the causal pairing argument is not a formidable challenge to divine interaction. It's not clear that there must be a pairing relation between God and material entities. But even if there were such a requirement, divine intentionality would plausibly fulfill that role.

2.4 Laws of Nature

Perhaps the most common objections to miracles is the claim that they would violate the laws of nature. This concept of miracles as "violations" has its roots in the Enlightenment, with thinkers such as Spinoza and Voltaire. However, it was David Hume's definition that had a lasting impact on the history of philosophy: miracles are "violations of the laws of nature by a deity" (2007: 83). Unfortunately, Hume himself did not elaborate on what exactly he thought the laws of nature were. Over the past century, however, Hume's definition, combined with a growing conviction about the immutability of the laws of nature, formed the basis of an argument against the possibility of miracles.[16]

For instance, speaking on behalf of the "modern age," Rudolf Bultmann declared that

> the idea of a miracle as divine intervention has become impossible for us today, because we understand all that happens in nature as law-governed. Thus we understand a miracle as a violation of the law-governed connection between all that happens in nature, and this idea we cannot entertain today any more." (quoted in von Wachter 2015: 39)

In addition, some contemporary theists believe that miracles, understood as divine interventions, don't occur. Nancey Murphy, for instance, objects "to interventionist accounts of divine action because it seems unreasonable that God should violate the laws he has established" (2000: 343).

---

[16] As we will see in Section 3, Hume himself did not think that his definition of the laws of nature implied that miracles were impossible.

What is wrong with interventionist models? The thought, following Murphy, is that God's intervention would violate laws of nature, which can't happen. However, since these theists do in fact believe that God has acted specially in history, they therefore go to great lengths to find a "noninterventionist" model of miracles according to which miracles do not violate the laws of nature. Some, for instance, suppose that God acts in the world by operating at the level of quantum mechanics (Russell 2008: 151–211). On this view, God causes certain quantum indeterministic states to collapse in such a way that, by means of chaos-theoretic amplifications, they have the macroscopic effects that God intends. The supposition is that no laws are violated because there are no deterministic laws at the quantum level.

In my view, there is some confusion about how this noninterventionist project is conceptualized. The root of the problem may be terminological. On this view, for God to *intervene* just means for him to violate some law of nature. But what the laws of nature are supposed to be – their metaphysical structure – is left unexplained.[17] It seems to me that those who engage in this project begin with an unclear and hazy notion of the laws of nature, proceed by assuming that intervention is incompatible with them, and are consequently forced to develop some noninterventionist model of divine action. This strikes me as backward. For God to intervene just means for him to act (Larmer 2021: 191–2). I therefore suggest the term "intervention" should be rescued in theological/philosophical discussions about special divine action. The real issue is not divine intervention, but rather the laws of nature. The incompatibility question is: what are the laws of nature such that divine intervention is supposedly at odds with them?

With this terminological clarification in place, we may return to our central point, which is to address an argument against miracles on the basis that they are violations of the laws of nature. Call this the No-Violation Argument. Its premises are as follows:

(1) If miracles occur, they violate the laws of nature.
(2) The laws of nature cannot be violated.

Therefore

(3) Miracles do not occur.

The problem with this argument, as I noted earlier, is that "the laws of nature" is ambiguous. In fact, there are several prominent models of the laws of nature

---

[17] Notice that we are not referring to "laws" as found in science textbooks (e.g., the laws of gravitation, of thermodynamics, Bernoulli's principle, Coulomb's law, and so forth). Rather, the question is about the essence of the laws – what they are in reality. In other words, it is a question of metaphysics, not physics.

defended by metaphysicians and philosophers of science. To assess the No-Violation Argument, we will examine these models to see if the argument succeeds on any of them.

2.4.1 Regularity Theories

As noted earlier, Hume himself didn't elaborate on what exactly the laws of nature are. Nevertheless, his more general views about causation eventually gave rise to what are known today as regularity theories of the laws of nature. On these theories, the laws of nature are (or describe) patterns of regularly occurring events in the world. It's a law of nature, for example, that electrons in proximity repel each other. Electrons display this behavior regularly and predictably. So, there is a law of nature concerning electrons.

Our universe, fortuitously, displays many regularities; hence, there are many laws of nature. Importantly, however, there is no necessitating relationship between these events. It's not that two electrons in proximity *must* or even *tend* to repel other electrons. Rather, they simply *do*: there is constant conjunction and nothing more. The laws of nature don't state what must happen but only what does happen. David Lewis compares the regularities in the world to a great mosaic (Lewis 1986: ix). From a distance, one can see patterns emerge in the mosaic. But these patterns are nothing more than the small pieces of glass scattered across a surface. Similarly, the patterns of events (qualities) in our universe may give the impression that there is some connecting relationship between them, but this is not so: the events themselves are modally disconnected. Nothing happens that necessitates that something else must happen. Now within the regularity view, we can distinguish two sub-positions: the exceptionless generalization view (EGV) and the best systems view (BSV). We will take each in turn.

2.4.2 The Exceptionless Generalization View (EGV)

The EGV, as its name implies, is the position that the laws of nature are universal generalizations that take the form "All Fs are Gs" and that hold true 100 percent of the time. Part of the motivation behind EGV is its empirical basis: we make empirical discoveries about the world and form generalizations about it. While a current generalization G may account for today's data (e.g., all dogs have four legs), we may find an exception tomorrow (e.g., we find a dog with three legs). Any exceptions are then incorporated into a new generalization G'. Ultimately, the aim is to pursue a universal generalization G* that tracks the regularities in the world without aberration (Popper 1992: 276).

Now, whatever its theoretical merits, EGV has been criticized to the extent that it is often dubbed the "naïve" regularity view. It's not my aim to rehearse these objections.[18] Instead, our question is: Does the No-Violation Argument succeed on EGV? Is there something about EGV that prohibits special divine acts?

Recall the premises of the argument:

(1) If miracles occur, they violate the laws of nature.
(2) The laws of nature cannot be violated.

Therefore

(3) Miracles do not occur.

Notice that premise (2) is correct by definition on EGV: the laws of nature are defined such that they are exceptionless. So, if one understands miracles as law violations, then miracles become impossible – but trivially so. In that case, however, if the theist accepts premise (2), she is free to reject premise (1). She might accept, in other words, that special divine acts take place in our universe but that such events *are parts of the laws of nature themselves*. There is nothing in the metaphysics of EGV itself to prevent divine intervention: if God were to intervene, then his actions would become part of the ultimate generalization G* that holds without exception. Of course, it may seem strange to suggest that miracles should be included in the laws of nature, and indeed so. But this oddity is the product of the way in which laws of nature are defined, not with the idea that God can intervene in the world. So, EGV poses no threat to miracles because the theist will reject premise (1).

2.4.3 The Best Systems View (BSV)

The BSV is a more nuanced version of the regularity theory (Ramsey 1928; Lewis 1973). According to BSV, not every regularity counts as a law of nature. Rather, the true laws of nature are the best systematizations of the regularities, where "best" is understood in terms of theoretical virtues such as simplicity and strength (Lewis 1973: 73). In other words, the laws of nature are those that invoke the fewest number of axioms while also accounting for the maximum number of events in the world. For instance, the statement "all dogs have four legs" is a plausible candidate as a law even if there are exceptions. Why? Because if statements about three-legged dogs were incorporated, then the resulting law would be more complex and ad hoc. So, BSV differs from EGV in that the laws are not necessarily exceptionless.

How should we understand the No-Violation Argument given BSV? The premises again are:

---

[18] See Mumford (2004: 31–40).

(1) If miracles occur, they violate the laws of nature.

(2) The laws of nature cannot be violated.

Given BSV, one option for the theist is to deny premise (2) and think of miracles as exceptions to the laws of nature. Richard Swinburne has defended a position roughly along these lines. Consider some miraculous event E and law of nature L as understood by the BSV. Swinburne explains that

> L will have to be retained as a law of nature and E regarded as a non-repeatable counter-instance to it, if any proposed rival formula L_1 were too much more complicated than L without giving better new predictions, or predicted new phenomena unsuccessfully where L predicted successfully. (1970: 29)

If this is correct, then nothing about BSV precludes miracles as long as the latter are understood as exceptions to the best system of regularities. It may be a law of nature that "deceased people don't rise from the dead," but if Jesus rises from the dead, this instance might be exceptional enough that it cannot be incorporated into that system.

We should also note in passing that the theist need not believe that God's activity is necessarily restricted to these exceptional instances. As far as logical possibilities go, God could intervene in nature in a regular, predictable manner that satisfies the conditions of being part of the best system of regularities (Archer 2015: 89–91). In fact, some Christians believe that God does perform miracles regularly and predicably: some, for instance, believe in transformation of bread and wine into the body and blood of Christ.[19] If we regard these as special divine acts, then they occur in a regular, predictable manner and under specified circumstances. Plausibly, then, they meet the criteria for being included in the best systematization of regularities. And if so, then a theist will also reject premise (1), for not all instances of special divine action need to be violations/exceptions to the laws. Therefore, given BSV, theists may reject premise (2) and perhaps even premise (1).

2.4.4 Second-Order Universals (SOU)

Some philosophers defend a view of the laws of nature according to which laws are second-order universals (SOU) (Armstrong 1983, 1997; Tooley 1987). To understand this position, consider two large physical bodies – say, the sun and the earth – which are attracted to each through a gravitational force. This attraction holds between any two objects with mass with a force proportional to the product of the masses divided by the square of the distance between them.

---

[19] See Aquinas (1956: ST III, q. 76, a. 8).

What explains or accounts for this behavior? The reason, according to proponents of SOU, is as follows. *Having mass* is a universal that an object instantiates.
Call this universal "M." There is another universal as well: *attracting other*
objects with mass. Call this universal "A." M and A are first-order universals.
But there is also a second-order universal N that makes it necessary that
whatever has M also has A. In other words, N *necessitates* that things that
have mass attract other things with mass. We can express the law thus: N(M, A).
So, in contrast to regularity theorists SOU proponents claim that there are
necessitating relations in the world. More generally, these necessitating relations take the form N(F, G) where F and G are first-order universals.

How might the No-Violation Argument run within the framework of SOU?
The argument, again, is:

(1) If miracles occur, they violate the laws of nature.
(2) The laws of nature cannot be violated.

We should first ask what a "violation" of a law of nature would be, given SOU.
We might initially suppose that a law of the form N(F, G) would be violated if
there were some entity with F that failed to instantiate G. Suppose that a boulder
is falling from a cliff onto innocent bystanders but that God intervenes to
suspend the boulder right before impact. Prima facie, this violates the gravitational law we referred to earlier, N(M, A), since we would then have an instance
in which the boulder (and the earth) has M but fails to exemplify A.

A closer analysis, however, reveals a different story. In fact, proponents of
SOU recognize that laws of the form N(F, G) do not always entail the exceptionless generalization, "all Fs are Gs." The reason is that the instantiation of
universals most often occurs in a context in which other laws of nature are at
work. David Armstrong explains:

> The entailment [that N(F, G) implies that all Fs are Gs] actually holds only for
> the cases where it is given that *nothing further interferes* ... [t]he situation is
> one that we are quite familiar with in scientific laws. The gravitational laws
> give the gravitational forces holding between two bodies having certain
> masses and at a certain distance from each other. It is not necessary that
> these forces cause the two bodies to move towards each other. There may be
> many other bodies also exerting gravitational force in the situation, not to
> mention other types of force ... The two bodies are caused to move towards
> each other according to the law that governs just two massive bodies *provided*
> *nothing else interferes.* (Armstrong 1997: 230, italics in original)

In other words, Armstrong notes that the laws of nature entail exceptionless
generalizations only in ideal circumstances – that is, when no external or
interfering forces are operating. And, of course, the theist will claim that

when God acts specially in the world, he is acting precisely as an external causal agent. As a result, premise one turns out to be false: miracles do not violate any laws since such laws do not entail exceptionless generalizations outside of idealized contexts. So, SOU poses no problem for special divine acts.[20]

2.4.5 Dispositional Essentialism

According to dispositional essentialism, the laws of nature supervene upon the dispositional nature of properties in the world (see Ellis 2002; Bird 2010). The laws of nature do not necessitate anything, nor do they do any "pushing" or "pulling" themselves. Rather, it is the properties of objects in the physical world that explain why natural entities behave as they do. These properties bestow specific dispositions upon their bearers.[21] For instance, a basketball has the disposition to bounce when thrown to the ground partly because it is round, made of rubber, has a certain weight, and so on. Given these dispositions, the presence of a stimulus (being thrown to the ground) yields a particular manifestation (its bouncing). More generally: having a property means being disposed to bring about a particular manifestation under certain stimulating conditions.

If we think of some disposition D, stimulus S, and manifestation M, then as an initial pass, the dispositional essentialist's claim is that:

(L) $\forall x\, ((Dx\, \&\, Sx) \rightarrow Mx).$

In other words, everything that has disposition D under a stimulus S exhibits manifestation M. But (L) is an initial pass only: upon reflection, we can see that (L) needs adjustment (Bird 2010: 59–60). There are circumstances in which a thing might have D under S but fail to bring about M. Consider, for instance, a glass vase with the dispositional property F, *being fragile*. Suppose that when the vase is struck by a hammer, the vase instantly heats up, thereby preventing it from breaking. Or, as another example, when the vase is struck, a powerful wizard casts a spell causing it to retain its rigidity (Lewis 1997: 147). In these cases, the disposition has been "finked": the vase is indeed fragile, but the

---

[20] Armstrong discusses the idea of "iron" laws – laws such that it is nomically (empirically) impossible that F be followed by anything other than G (1997: 231). But theists will claim that even if it is nomically impossible for F to yield G, God's actions are not restricted by nomic necessity. Fales adopts a variation of the SOU according to which the relation between first-order universals is metaphysically necessary. He maintains, however, that the instantiation of A does not always require the instantiation of B (2010: 163n16). Instead, A "contributes" to the production of B under certain conditions. The theist can argue, however, that God may also be a causal contributor, meaning that no laws are violated through divine interventions.

[21] The "essentialism" in dispositional essentialism refers to the fact that properties have their dispositions as part of their essence: there is no possible world in which electrons have the property *being negatively charged* yet lack the disposition to repel other electrons.

disposition does not bring about its typical manifestation because of some extraneous factor. Another example: hemlock has the property *being deadly when ingested*. But suppose that when Socrates drinks the hemlock, he immediately takes an antidote. As a result, he does not die. In this case, the antidote serves as a "mask" for the hemlock such that although the poison has the property *being deadly when ingested*, the manifestation is never produced. In other words, what is needed to correct (L) is to incorporate a *ceteris paribus* clause (Bird 2010: 60):

(L') [$\forall x$ ((Dx & Sx) $\rightarrow$ Mx), in the absence of finks and masks.].

We now have a more plausible formulation of dispositional essentialist laws since, as in the case of Armstrong's SOU, one must also account for external factors interfering with the usual manifestations of properties.

Let us return now to the No-Violation Argument:

(1) If miracles occur, they violate the laws of nature.
(2) The laws of nature cannot be violated.

It's difficult to say what would constitute a violation of the laws of nature on the dispositional essentialist view. The reason is that the laws, as we have seen, have *ceteris paribus* clauses; they describe what happens in the absence of external influences.[22] In any case, the theist may deny premise (1) as she did in the SOU view. If God acts specially in the world, his actions are a source of change beyond the dispositional properties possessed by objects. One might even think of some miracles in terms of finks and masks (Archer 2015: 92–5). An example is this: when humans die, their bodies have the disposition to remain dead, to decompose, and so forth. And the laws of nature reflect this fact: dead bodies have the disposition to stay dead – but only in the absence of finks and masks. But just as Lewis's wizard casts a spell to keep a vase from manifesting its disposition to break on impact, so God might change the structure of Jesus' corpse so that its usual manifestations (e.g., to remain dead) are masked. Of course, a theist need not claim that finks and masks are the only means of special divine activity. The point is only that premise (1) of the No-Violation Argument is false when the laws of nature are understood in the way described by dispositional essentialists.

---

[22] Another option along these lines is to suggest that laws of nature do not have *ceteris paribus* clauses. Instead, the laws describe "tendencies" – for example, the tendency of a massive object to attract other such objects (gravity). These tendencies continue to operate even if overriding forces are present, and thus no laws are violated. For a theory that grounds tendencies in states of affairs rather than dispositions or powers, see Von Wachter (2015).

2.4.6 Lawless Causal Powers

Finally, some defend the position that there are no laws of nature (Mumford 2004). According to this view, entities in the world have intrinsic causal powers or abilities, and their behavior is the result of the exercise of those powers. For instance, billiard balls have certain properties – being round, being solid, and so on. Consider the property *being round*. Causal powers theorists claim that having such a property *just is* a causal power that the ball possesses. Because it is round, a billiard ball has the ability to roll along a surface when the right conditions are in place. We can generalize: things in the universe have causal powers that can be exercised, and the exercise of those powers results in the natural behavior we observe, which forms the basis of scientific inquiry. It is false, however, that there are laws of nature "out there" that govern the behavior of things hereabouts. Instead, the causal powers of objects suffice to account for the activity of natural entities without having to invoke any laws.[23]

The No-Violation Argument clearly does not apply to this view since there are no laws of nature to be violated in the first place. If God chooses to act specially in the world, his actions will intervene in the nexus of causal powers in the universe. There is no abstract law or laws that would prohibit special divine acts.

Summary

We have seen that the No-Violation Argument is more complex than its advocates often recognize. The simplicity of Hume's definition might incline someone toward an easy dismissal of miracles without specifying exactly what the laws of nature are. However, we've examined five models of the laws of nature and have concluded that the argument against miracles gains traction on none of them.

2.5 What Are Miracles?

We are now able to offer a more robust definition or characterization of a miracle. My own inclination is to drop any reference to the laws of nature in a definition of a miracle. Part of the reason is that I'm inclined to accept what the last two views in the foregoing discussion have in common, namely that the source of behavior among natural entities is their intrinsic dispositions or powers.

This seems to get us the right result. As Timothy McGrew points out, "One benefit of defining miracles in terms of violations of natural law is that this

---

[23] In this respect, the causal powers theorists and dispositional essentialists have similar metaphysical commitments. However, dispositional essentialists stop short of eliminating laws altogether. See Bird (2010: 189–203).

definition entails that a miracle is beyond the productive power of nature. But if that is the key idea, then it is hard to see why we should not simply use that as the definition and leave out the problematic talk of laws" (2014: section 1.2). Of course, our previous discussion about the laws of nature might prove valuable to those who embrace regularity theories, SOU views, or otherwise.

In addition, recall from Section 1 that I have already offered a partial definition of special divine actions. I suggested that miracles are acts of God that go beyond his creation of the world, his conserving it in existence, and his concurrence with secondary causes. After this section's discussion, we can add more to this characterization: miracles are divine acts that exceed the causal powers found in nature. Waters and winds by themselves lack the power to divide the Red Sea. Three-day-old corpses lack the capacity to rise to life once again. Yet these are possible with external intervention. So, *miracles are acts of God in the universe that are (i) beyond divine creation, conservation, and concurrence, and that (ii) exceed the causal powers of natural entities.*[24]

Notice that I have been using the term "miracle" and "special divine action" interchangeably. Accordingly, while there may be non-divine sources of causal influence beyond nature (angels, demons, souls, etc.) these do not count as miracles properly speaking.[25] Moreover, my definition restricts miracles to the natural world. If there are instances of divine activity outside the universe (e.g., in heaven, between the persons of the Trinity), these do not qualify as miracles.

Some may object, however, that our definition has an important lacuna, namely it does not account for the surprising, unanticipated dimension of miracles. David Basinger, for instance, characterizes a miracle as "an unusual, unexpected, observable event due in part to the intentional direct interventive activity of God" (2018: 17; also see Larmer 2013: 32). I agree that the miracles described in the Bible do often have this unexpected character (though perhaps not always – think of the expected, regular fall of manna in the desert).

On the other hand, it seems to me that such conditions should not be included in the definition of special divine acts. The "unexpected" condition, for instance, is purely epistemic. Suppose Mother Teresa prays for the instantaneous healing of a child, while fully expecting the miracle to take place. If God acts in response to her prayer and heals the child, does the event fail to be

---

[24] For definitions in the same ballpark, see Larmer (2013: 32), McGrew (2014, section 1.3), Von Wachter (2015), Luck (2016: 271), and Aquinas (1956: ST I q. 105 a. 7; ST I q. 110 a. 4).

[25] Of course, one is free to assign the label "miracle" to some supernatural event brought about by a non-divine source. If so, however, then the phenomenon in question is outside the scope of this Element, which is restricted to divine actions.

a miracle because it was expected? Alternatively, suppose the parents of the sick child did not expect divine intervention. Was the healing a miracle for them but not for Mother Teresa? Miracles, it seems to me, are not person-relative in this way.

Similar considerations apply to the "unusual" condition. It's possible that miracles might occur in a usual, regular fashion. Consider a clock that operates with rotating gears. Suppose that one of the "teeth" of the gears is damaged: it is cracked in such a way that would normally prevent the clock from functioning. But suppose in addition that at every turn of the gear God intervenes to keeps the broken tooth intact. Thus, the clock ticks away indefinitely. In this example, God intervenes usually and regularly, yet it seems to be a clear instance (or series of instances) of special divine activity.

These considerations suggest that a definition of miracles should not contain the condition that they are unexpected, irregular, unusual, or the like. It may be *contingently* true that God intervenes in the world unexpectedly and irregularly, but this manner of acting would not be an essential component of special divine actions.

2.6 Conclusion

The primary goal of this section has been to address anti-miracle objections stemming from principles commonly associated with science and scientific discourse. We saw that the causal closure of the physical, despite the enormous confidence often placed in it, lacks any compelling justification. As an empirical claim, it fails to be supported by inductive evidence that would exclude instances of divine intervention. The conservation of energy principle applies only to closed systems and is not equivalent to the claim that "energy can neither be created nor destroyed," which in any case is a metaphysical proposition, not a scientific one. The causal pairing problem assumes either that pairing relations are necessary for causation or that God cannot be paired with material objects. We saw that both assumptions are plausibly false. Finally, we examined five metaphysical models of the laws of nature, and I suggested that the No-Violation Argument fails on all of them. In the end, I proposed that a proper definition of a miracle should drop any mention of the laws of nature and focus instead on intrinsic dispositions or causal powers.

3 Miracles and Justified Belief

In Sections 1 and 2, we made progress in clarifying the nature of special divine actions and responding to various theological, scientific, and metaphysical arguments against them. It is important to note, however, that these arguments aimed to undermine the *possibility* of miracles. In this section, I address a different kind of objection. This type of argument suggests that *even if* miracles are possible, we can never be rationally justified in believing them on the basis of the testimony of others. This section, in other words, is about the epistemology of miracles.

3.1 Hume's Argument

It is difficult to overstate the impact and influence of David Hume's essay "On Miracles." Scholars across academic fields, particularly in theology and biblical studies, often employ Hume's reasoning, whether or not they are aware of the Scottish philosopher's influence.

Hume has been subject to varied interpretations by later scholars.[26] There is consequently a meta-level interpretive debate about Hume and the precise formulation of his arguments. Although such debates are interesting, they are not the focus of this section. Instead, I engage with a fairly mainstream interpretation that matches my own.

Hume starts his lengthy treatment of miracles by outlining what he considers to be evidence in general. Given his empiricist commitment to ground rational justification in experience, he frames evidence in terms of observations, or what he calls "experiments." Suppose we are trying to guess the likelihood of some event, such as the sun's rising tomorrow. To do so, we must recall past experiences and observations: how many times have we seen the sun rise in the past, and how many times haven't we? The wise man, says Hume,

> weighs opposite experiments. He considers which side is supported by the greater number of experiments: To that side he inclines, without doubt and hesitation; and when at last he fixes his judgment, the evidence exceeds not what we properly called *probability*. All probability, then supposes an opposition of experiments and observations, where the one side is found to overbalance the other, and to produce a degree of evidence proportioned to that superiority. (2007: 80, italics in original)

Evidence, in other words, is expressed in terms of probabilities, and probabilities in turn are based on events that have been observed in the past. What is the likelihood that the sun will rise tomorrow? It is extremely high (though never 100 percent) since we have observed plenty of sunrises and nothing to the contrary.[27]

---

[26] Earman attributes much of the interpretive disagreement to Hume himself: "I defy the reader to give a short, simple, and accurate summary of the argumentation in 'Of Miracles.' What on first reading appears to be a seamless argument is actually a collection of considerations that sometimes mesh and sometimes don't" (2000: 20).

[27] This is the "problem of induction" that Hume made famous.

Hume applies this general evidential framework to beliefs that are based on *testimony*. This is the way that many, if not most, people have believed in miracles, namely because others have reported them (e.g., the miracles of Jesus recounted in the Gospels). In such cases, we do not directly observe miracles ourselves: all we have are the (purported) observations of other people. So how do we assess the weight of testimonial evidence when it comes to miracles?

Hume first notes that just because someone *claims* to have witnessed a miracle does not mean that the claim is true. Errors of memory, tendencies toward exaggerations, malicious intentions, and other factors can contribute to inaccuracies in miracle reports. As a result, there is no necessary connection between the *reports* of miracles and the *truth* of those reports. We must therefore weigh, assess, and evaluate the claims of testimony just as we would any other kind of claims: by examining past observations.

Hume envisions a kind of tug-of-war between competing factors. For example, suppose my friend tells me he saw a white deer wandering in the woods. However, I've gone to the woods every day for twenty years and have never seen a white deer. In addition, after reading a book on the subject, I learn that white deer are not native to my geographical area. At this point, Hume's empiricism gains traction. Based on observation, both my own and that of the book's authors/sources, should I believe my friend? After all, people often misreport events, and there could be other explanations, such as that my friend has made a mistake or is playing a practical joke. Therefore, the weight of my friend's testimony should diminish in proportion to the overwhelming observations that go against it.[28]

Now let us return to miracles. As we saw in Section 2, Hume defines a miracle as a "violation of the laws of nature." We must be careful, however, about misinterpreting Hume here. Hume is not arguing that miracles are impossible, nor is he mounting an argument against miracles based on his metaphysical views about the laws of nature. Instead, he is concerned with epistemology. When Hume refers to "laws of nature," he means all the events that have been repeatedly observed in the past and that are formed by "firm and unalterable experience" (2004: 83). He is therefore suggesting that it is impossible to justify a belief in a miracle based on testimony, since the evidence against a miracle will always be overwhelmingly stronger. Hume declares:

> Nothing is esteemed a miracle, if it ever happens in the common course of nature. It is no miracle that a man, seemingly in good health, should die on a sudden: because such a kind of death, though more unusual than any other, has yet been frequently observed to happen. But it is a miracle, that a dead

---

[28] Technically, the information gathered through my book would also count as testimonial evidence. Let this pass, however, since as we will see, Hume does entertain the idea that miracles go against uniform experience, which includes the experience of others.

man should come to life; because that has never been observed, in any age or country. There must, therefore, be a uniform experience against every miraculous event, otherwise the event would not merit that appellation. And as a uniform experience amounts to a proof, there is here a direct and full *proof*, from the nature of the fact, against the existence of any miracle; nor can such a proof be destroyed, or the miracle rendered credible, but by an opposite proof, which is superior. (2004: 83)

This passage contains several points worth noting. First, Hume appears to be begging the question when he claims that resurrections have "never been observed, in any age or country." However, we should interpret Hume charitably here by keeping in mind that he does allow for the possibility of miracles *in principle*. By extension, we should therefore assume he would allow the possibility that someone might observe miracles, even if he believes that the truth of miracle claims can never be rationally established through the testimony of others.

Second, it might be tempting to think that by "full proof" Hume means that uniform experience establishes a probability of one against miracles. I will say more about probabilities, but for now we should note that Hume likely does not mean "full proof" in this way (though he can be unclear on this). The reason is that in the same passage, he seems to entertain at least the possibility of an opposite "superior" proof, and it's unclear what sort of proof would be superior to a full proof. Therefore, what Hume means is that uniform experience establishes an *extremely high* probability against miraculous testimony, such that realistically no claim to the contrary can outweigh it.

From this reasoning, Hume concludes with his famous maxim:

"That no testimony is sufficient to establish a miracle, unless the testimony be of such a kind, that its falsehood would be more miraculous, than the fact, which it endeavours to establish: And even in that case there is a mutual destruction of arguments and the superior only gives us an assurance suitable to that degree of force, which remains, after deducting the inferior." When any one tells me, that he saw a dead man restored to life, I immediately consider with myself, whether it be more probable, that this person should either deceive or be deceived, or that the fact, which he relates should really have happened. I weigh the one miracle against the other; and according to the superiority, which I discover, I pronounce my decision, and always reject the greater miracle. (2004: 83)

This is the culmination of the tug-of-war. Uniform experience and observations will always emerge victorious. Whatever testimonial evidence there may be in favor of a miraculous claim, it is overwhelmingly more probable that the testimony is mistaken. Indeed, if we are to believe some testimony about a miracle, the evidential weight in its favor needs to be so extraordinary, so overwhelming, that it would be more "miraculous" – what he means here is more *improbable* – that the event did not occur.

Let us call this line of reasoning the "first phase" of Hume's argument. He then quickly moves on to a "second phase." So far, he has allowed that, in principle, there may be *some* weight behind testimonial reports even though he believes such reports, in any case, will never surmount the unlikelihood of the miracle itself. In the second phase, Hume attempts to bolster his case by claiming that testimonial reports of miracles have in fact always been weak. I will develop these arguments in greater detail later. For now, here is a summary of the four arguments he advances.

First, no miracle has ever been attested by credible people – those who are educated, sensible, have much to lose if their claims turn out to be false, and can present their case publicly. Second, humans tend to invent or mistakenly infer miracles because such events strike them as surprising, wonderful, and marvelous – all of which generate positive emotions. Third, miracle claims "are observed chiefly to abound among ignorant and barbarous nations" (2004: 86). Purported miraculous activity tends to occur far away from us. Finally, miracles take place within the context of conflicting religious systems. Miracle claims are supposed to vindicate one religion or over another, but all equally claim to be backed by miracles. According to Hume, both sets of miracle claims are therefore discredited.

This completes the second phase of Hume's argument. Taking a step back, we can see that Hume's case against miracles has several moving pieces. There is the conviction that miracles are intrinsically improbable events ("otherwise the event would not merit that appellation"). There is also the claim that miracle reports should be assessed based on previous experience and observations. These are to be weighed against the likelihood that the reports are the products of misperceptions or deceit. Finally, Hume offers a cumulative case argument aimed at diminishing our confidence in miracle claims more generally.

3.2 Hume Reconsidered

Despite the popularity of Hume's essay, his account has several important deficits. Some of these were recognized by philosophers during Hume's own time, and contemporary philosophers have brought many of these problems into clearer focus.

3.2.1 Frozen Rivers

The first phase of Hume's argument attempts to show that uniform experience (by way of empirical observation) always trumps testimonial evidence for miracles. The likelihood of a false report about miracles is always greater than likelihood that we have found an exception to our universal experience.

There are a couple of ways to respond to this argument. First, applying Hume's principle to improbable events in general makes the principle vulnerable to counterexamples. And given that there are counterexamples to this more generalized principle, we must ask whether there is anything about miracles *in particular* that renders them susceptible to Hume's argument.

Consider the following example, which Hume himself wrestles with. Imagine a prince who lives in a hot climate year-round and has never seen frozen water. An explorer returns from a distant land and reports to the prince that during his travels, he has witnessed ice – in fact, entire rivers that are completely frozen. Should the prince believe the explorer?

Hume seems to suggest that the prince's initial skepticism is justified. He nevertheless claims that "very strong" testimony would be sufficient for the prince to believe the report (2004: 82). This immediately places Hume in an awkward position. Evidently, there are cases in which testimony can ground beliefs in improbable events that have uniform experience against them. But then why not allow miracles the same courtesy? In other words, Hume's argument against belief in miracles appears to be too strong and excludes improbable events that we think testimonial evidence may overturn.

To salvage his argument, Hume has at least two moves at his disposal. In the context of the prince example, one rejoinder is to claim that although the prince had uniform experience against frozen water in his own country, there was not uniform experience against frozen water in *all circumstances*, including the other country. In other words, there are two types of uniform experience. One is local uniform experience, which is restricted to the prince's own personal history of observations and perceptions. The other is global uniform experience, which includes the observations and perceptions of everyone, including those of the explorer and the inhabitants of the colder country. For an event to be properly "contrary to experience," it must have global uniform experience against it. Miraculous events fall into this category. By contrast, *marvelous* events such as frozen rivers are not contrary to the prince's experience. They are simply not "conformable" to it (2004: 82). Thus, the prince's initial skepticism about frozen water may be overturned by testimony since frozen water, in Hume's terminology, is merely a marvelous event but not a miraculous one.

This response will convince few anti-skeptics. The latter have an easy rebuttal: they will simply argue that miracles fall into our global uniform experience even if they are not part of the skeptic's local uniform experience. In other words, it's not enough simply to affirm that "dead men don't rise" is a proposition backed by *everyone's* experience. Recall that Hume himself remains open to the possibility that miracles occur. However, if we cannot rule out a priori that miracles have taken place, then we cannot rule out a priori that they are not part of our global uniform experience. If that's the case, then we must be open to the possibility that testimonial evidence could justify belief in miracles, just as it justified the prince's belief in frozen rivers.

Hume has another possible response. He may argue that the prince is justified in believing the report of frozen water because the latter has certain "analogies" with familiar phenomena. For example, the prince has observed that water vapor can change into liquid, and that other liquids (such as liquid metal) become solid when cooled. Therefore, by reasoning from analogy, the prince can conclude that frozen water is not "contrary to his experience," even if he hasn't observed it himself.

Again, however, this response is unlikely to persuade many anti-skeptics. The concept of an "analogy" in this context is notoriously vague. What level of similarity is required for two concepts to be considered analogous? In any case, anti-skeptics may simply assert that many miracles do in fact have relevant analogies. For example, regarding resurrections, we have observed that bodily tissue can repair itself, that individuals can transition from being unconscious to conscious, and that cases of clinical death can sometimes be reversed. If there are differences in similarity between frozen river analogies and resurrection analogies, they are at best a matter of degree, not of kind. The skeptic must provide a non-question-begging way of showing why certain analogies are legitimate while others are not.

3.2.2 Distinguishing Probabilities

Hume's attempt to demonstrate that some claims about unseen phenomena (such as frozen rivers) may be accepted on the basis of testimony, while others (such as miracles) cannot, is unconvincing. Nevertheless, this does not completely resolve the issue. One could still argue that Hume should have stood by his initial verdict: that the prince was not justified in believing in frozen rivers based on testimony.

This brings us to the crux of Hume's argument, which is ultimately about *probabilities*. Recall that Hume characterizes a miracle as an enormously *improbable* event, one that goes against uniform experience. Otherwise, it would not "merit that appellation." The claim that we must confront is this: even if miracles have occurred in the past, they are overwhelmingly rare. Although one dead person may have come back to life 2,000 years ago, the vast majority of dead people have stayed dead. The sheer number of times that nature has followed its course without special divine intervention creates a probabilistic "mountain" that must be overcome to justify belief in miracles.

Testimonial evidence may help ascend this mountain, but it can go only so far. Humans frequently report falsehoods, either intentionally or unintentionally, and it appears that false reports occur much more frequently than miracles. It seems, therefore, that the odds are always against miracle reports.

Up until now, I have been using terms such as "probability," "odds," and "likelihood" somewhat loosely; we should now try to be more precise. In particular, we should distinguish between two types of probabilities: (i) the probability of an event given our general background knowledge of the world alone and (ii) the probability of an event given *both* our background knowledge *and* the evidence in favor of that event. These are respectively known as an event's "prior probability" and its "posterior probability."[29]

To illustrate, consider a criminal case: the murder of Bob, who has been stabbed to death. Adam, an acquaintance of Bob with no criminal record, works at the same large company. Suppose that is all we know about the situation. These facts form our background knowledge. If we ask ourselves, "What is the probability that Adam murdered Bob, based solely on this background knowledge?" the answer will presumably be "very low." But suppose we learn additional information. Adam and Bob were last seen having a heated dispute at work the day before the murder. When investigators reached Adam's house, they found a large, bloody knife on his kitchen counter. These discoveries increase the probability we assign to the hypothesis that Adam murdered Bob. Of course, they do not absolutely settle the matter (Adam might be innocent after all), but the point is that we are assessing two types of probabilities. The initial likelihood that Adam murdered Bob based on our background knowledge alone is the prior probability. The resulting likelihood that Adam murdered Bob based on our background knowledge plus the new evidence is the posterior probability.

Probability theorists over the past few centuries have studied the way that probabilities change in the presence of new evidence. An important equation used in this context is Bayes's theorem, named after the philosopher and statistician Thomas Bayes (1701–61). It will help make our discussion more precise.

Let $P(X/Y)$ stand for the "probability of X given Y," and let H stand for the hypothesis in question, E stand the evidence for that hypothesis, and K stand for one's background knowledge of the world. Bayes's theorem can be formulated as follows.

---

[29] Here I have subjective probabilities in mind instead of objective probabilities. The difference between the two is that subjective probabilities measure a person's degree of belief based on her own background knowledge whereas objective probabilities are probabilities in the real world, independent of personal judgments.

$$P(H/E\&K) = \frac{P(H/K) * P(E/K\&H)}{P(E/K)}$$

The left side of the equation, P(H/E&K), is the aforementioned posterior probability. This is the probability that we are interested in, namely the probability that the hypothesis is true given both our background knowledge of the world and the evidence for the hypothesis. The first factor in the numerator on the right side, P(H/K), is the prior probability. It expresses the odds of the hypothesis based *solely* on our background knowledge of the world. The next factor, P(E/K&H), called the *likelihood*, measures how well the hypothesis explains the evidence in question. Finally, the denominator, P(E/K), is called the *expectancy* of E. It measures how much we would expect the evidence in the first place based on our background knowledge alone.

Bayes's theorem has a wide range of practical applications, such as calculating the probabilities of false positives in medical diagnostics, the probability of the inheritance of genetic traits, and financial probabilities in the stock market. In other words, it is not simply the brainchild of speculative philosophers and mathematicians!

If we translate Hume's reasoning in terms of the probability statements in Bayes's theorem, we end up with the following. Hume wants to demonstrate that the posterior probability, P(H/E&K), of a miracle is low. Given Bayes's theorem, there are two ways to do this.

(1) *Show that the prior probability of the miracle is low* (i.e., show that P(H/K) is low). This is the burden of much of Hume's argument, since he suggests that uniform experience weighs against miracles.

(2) *Show that the evidence of the reports is weak* (i.e., show that P(E/K&H)/P(E/K) is low). If we can demonstrate that the evidence would likely be the same whether or not the miracle occurred, then the evidence is relatively weak.

The debate between skeptics and anti-skeptics fundamentally surrounds these two points. The more one can establish both (1) and (2), the lower the posterior probability of the miracle. Conversely, if one fails to demonstrate (1) or (2), then the argument against miracles loses its force. In the following two subsections, I examine each of these claims individually.

3.2.3 Prior Probabilities

Consider (1), the attempt to establish that the prior probability of a miracle is low. We saw that Hume assigns an infinitesimally low prior probability to miracles because miracles violate the laws of nature, which are established by "a firm and unalterable experience." Now, as an interpretive point, we should not think that Hume maintains the prior probability of a miracle is low *on the basis that no one has ever witnessed a miracle*. This would make the argument circular. Rather, Hume's claim is about the general human experience: people generally don't claim to have witnessed miracles or to have experienced healings. In the grand scheme of things, these are relatively rare, and in any case, according to Hume, they usually come from less-educated and underdeveloped parts of the world. Miracle reports are not part of the general human experience across the board.

However, one may challenge this judgment. Studies suggest that miracle claims are far more prevalent than Hume thought. For example, a 2006 Pew Research survey in ten countries (United States, Brazil, Chile, Guatemala, Kenya, Nigeria, South Africa, India, the Philippines, and South Korea) found that on average, 73 percent of Pentecostals, 52 percent of charismatics, and 39 percent of "other Christians" claimed to have experienced or witnessed a divine healing of an illness or injury (Pew Research, 2006; Keener, 2011: 239). Given the population of these countries, this translates to hundreds of millions of people who claim to have witnessed firsthand at least one divine healing. This number would be even larger if more countries had been included in the survey.

Although most miracle claims are undocumented, some are. In a two-volume work on miracles, Craig Keener provides meticulous documentation of hundreds of contemporary miracle reports. These reports include instantaneous healings from blindness, paralysis, and terminal illnesses, as well as exorcisms and various nature miracles. Keener offers detailed reports from eyewitnesses, medical documentation, and other corroborative evidence. These miracle claims come from around the globe, not only from developing countries but also in many technologically advanced societies.

To be clear, my intention in citing the Pew Research Center and Keener's work is not to demonstrate that any or some miracle claims are veridical. Rather, the point is to contest Hume's conviction that a "firm and unalterable experience" against miracles is an accurate representation of what we find in the world. Insofar as Hume establishes the low prior probability of miracles inductively based on this judgment, the anti-skeptic has grounds to reject it.

A second way of challenging the infinitesimally low prior probability of miracles is by considering the implications of God as their cause, as well as the context in which miracle claims are made. Many miracle reports seem improbable because, as even the anti-skeptic grants, God typically does not intervene specially in the regular patterns of natural behavior. Boulders usually fall off cliffs unimpeded, and dead people generally remain dead. However, there may be circumstances in which one might reasonably anticipate God's intervention, particularly in situations of heightened religious significance (a topic we will discuss in Section 4). In other words, there may be cases in which our background knowledge of the world changes the prior probability we would otherwise assign to a miraculous event.

Consider a more general example. The probability that any given person will receive a personal visit from Lionel Messi, the great Argentine football star, is extremely low. He doesn't usually visit random people. But let's suppose we have additional information. Messi is known to visit children in hospitals who are suffering from physical illnesses, especially those related to growth hormone deficiencies (since he himself had such a condition when he was younger). Suppose we also know that a pediatric hospital in Barcelona specializes in treating children with such conditions, and that Messi lives in Barcelona, near this hospital. In such a case, we can reasonably assume that the probability that a patient at this hospital will receive a visit from Messi is much higher than the probability that any random person will receive a visit from him.

Similarly, in some cases, we might reasonably think that God has unique reasons for intervening in the world. For example, suppose we believe that God has specially aligned himself with the nation of Israel throughout history. Additionally, we learn about Jesus of Nazareth, whose ethical teachings and conduct reflect what we consider to be the character of this God. Moreover, suppose we also believe that Jesus proclaimed himself to be the unique revelation of Israel's God in history, and that he predicted his own ignominious death and subsequent restoration to life. In such a case, it might be reasonable to assume that Jesus "fits the profile" of someone on behalf of whom God would perform a miracle. Given this new background information, we might come to believe that the likelihood of God's raising Jesus *in particular* from the dead is higher (although not necessarily high) than it would be for many other people.[30]

In sum, we have reason to doubt the first Humean contention that the prior probability of miracles is always so infinitesimally low that it creates a sort of mountain of evidence that a miracle claim can never overcome. I have argued that, in some cases, this mountain may not be as tall as Hume supposes.

3.2.4 The Weight of Evidence

Let us consider the second way the skeptic may argue for the low (posterior) probability of a miracle. This strategy is to demonstrate that the evidence, in the form of testimony, is weak. If one can show that we would expect our current evidence, whether or not the miracle actually occurred, then such evidence

---

[30] Swinburne (2003: 32–141) gives an extended argument along these lines.

carries little weight. In that case, the presence of the testimony would do relatively little to change our assessment of the miracle's prior probability.

To his credit, Hume acknowledges that testimony may have at least some evidential power. Most of what we believe comes from the reports of others. For example, your coworker tells you that he went skiing over the weekend for the first time in his life. You believe him, and justifiably so, without the need to uncover physical evidence that he was there or to call his wife for corroboration (which would be a form of testimony anyway).

The real question, then, is about the quality of testimonial evidence supporting miracle claims. Hume's "second phase" (which corresponds roughly to the second part of his essay) can be seen as his attempt to downplay the strength of the actual evidence for miracles. Earlier in this section, I provided a summary of these arguments, and I will now expand on them.

Hume's first argument is this:

> [T]here is not to be found, in all of history, any miracle attested by a sufficient number of men, of such unquestionable good-sense, education, and learning, as to secure us against all delusion in themselves; of such undoubted integrity, as to place them beyond any suspicion of any design to deceive others . . . as to have a great deal to lose in the case of their being detected in any falsehood; and at the same time, attesting facts, performed in such a public manner, in so celebrated a part of the world, as to render the detection unavoidable: All which circumstances are requisite to give us a full assurance in the testimony of man. (2004: 84)

In the last sentence, Hume seems to claim that these conditions are necessary to establish "full assurance" in a miracle claim. Full assurance, however, if understood as compelling or complete evidence, is more than the anti-skeptic needs. Plausible or strong evidence (evidence that would overturn the lower prior probability attached to the miracle) might be enough, even if that evidence is not overwhelming. If a miracle claim were to meet all Hume's conditions except, for example, that it took place somewhere in the world that is not "celebrated" – whatever that means – wouldn't that still constitute strong evidence in its favor?

Of course, taken individually, some of these principles are unimpeachable: having more witnesses attesting to a miraculous event is better than having fewer witnesses, all else being equal. If the witnesses have much to lose if they are revealed as liars, this adds evidential weight. Other principles are more suspect. For example, what exactly is "unquestionable good-sense, education, and learning"? The terms, as commonly used, are hardly synonymous: many well-educated people lack good sense, and vice versa. Does this education contain an inherent skeptical posture toward miracles? Such a condition strikes me as too vague to carry much significance in the debate about miracles.

Furthermore, those who offer evidence for miracles often affirm that many of these conditions are met. For instance, those who argue for the resurrection of Jesus often point out that the alleged initial eyewitnesses of the resurrection had little to gain for lying. What awaited them for following a crucified messianic pretender was persecution, martyrdom, and, for them, condemnation before God himself. Another argument involves highlighting that the reports attesting to the resurrection are found in multiple, independent sources, and that the descriptions of the resurrection were public in nature (1 Cor. 15:3–8; Matt. 28:9–10, 16–20; Luke 24:13–43; John 21:1–19). Analyzing such arguments in detail goes beyond the scope of this Element.[31] The point is simply that anti-skeptics in many cases will affirm that certain miracle claims do meet some of the conditions laid out by Hume.

In Hume's second argument, he claims:

> The passion of *suprize* and *wonder*, arising from miracles, being an agreeable emotion, gives a sensible tendency towards the belief of those events, from which it is derived … But if the spirit of religion join itself to the love of wonder, there is an end of common sense; and human testimony, in these circumstances, loses all pretentions to authority. (2004: 84–5).

Hume argues further that this desire for surprise and wonder is evident when we consider the great number of forged miracles, deceptions, and failed prophecies.

Hume's suggestion seems to be that because human beings are predisposed to accept miracles, this somehow discredits or constitutes evidence against claims in their favor. However, attraction toward the marvelous, the beautiful, and outstanding need not denigrate beliefs that result from such inclinations. This is also the case in other disciplines. For example, scientific investigation and discourse are often driven by aesthetic considerations, and mathematicians may pursue theories because they find them elegant or enlightening.[32] At most, Hume's point here should serve as a healthy reminder to exercise circumspection when investigating miracle claims.

Furthermore, if theism is true, then it shouldn't come as a surprise that humans are attracted or drawn to miracles. One of the central tenets of monotheistic religions is that God created human beings to be in fellowship with himself.[33] As I will argue in Section 4, miracles may function as signs that direct people to God. If so, then the positive emotions that arise from miracle claims may be an aspect

---

[31] On this, see Craig (1989), Swinburne (2003), Wright (2003), and Licona (2010). For a sympathetic but more skeptical take, see Allison (2021).

[32] Regarding science, see Ivanova and French (2022). Regarding mathematics, Gian-Carlo Rota notes, "If the statements of mathematics were merely formally true but in no way enlightening, then mathematics would be no more than a curious game played by some weird people" (1997: 181).

[33] In the opening lines of his *Confessions*, Augustine famously exclaims to God that "you have made us and drawn us to yourself, and our heart is unquiet until it rests in you" (2012: 39).

of proper human functioning. For the objection to succeed, Hume would have to provide a refutation of theism, which is not his aim.[34]

In his third argument, Hume claims that miracles "are observed chiefly to abound among ignorant and barbarous nations" (2004: 86). Unlike "wise and learned" people (presumably in Hume's circle), "[f]ools are industrious in propagating the imposture." Further, such specious miracle reports originate and thrive in "ignorant and barbarous" countries because "[n]one of their countrymen have a large correspondence, or sufficient credit and authority to contradict and beat down the delusion" (87).

This argument has aged poorly, partly because Hume's terminology is strident to modern ears. We should interpret Hume charitably, however, and remember that such language was a product of the age. His concern is to draw attention to the differences in education and technology between Hume's own country and those of others during his time. The real problem with the argument is its assumption that better education or a more advanced society will naturally produce a skeptical outlook. On the contrary, many developing countries today are far more educationally and technologically advanced than were eighteenth-century Scotland and England. Yet surveys from such countries (see the Pew Research study cited earlier) show that belief in miracles abound in these places. So, this argument is unpersuasive.

Hume's final argument is about miracles in competing religious systems. He declares that "there is no testimony for any [miracle] ... that is not opposed by an infinite number of witnesses; so that not only the miracle destroys the credit of testimony, but the testimony destroys itself" (2004: 87). The idea here is that religious systems are necessarily opposed to each other: "in matters of religion, whatever is different is contrary" (88). Yet, says Hume, most religions employ miracle claims in order to validate themselves over others. The resulting situation is a sort of "canceling out" of miracles claims.

There are at least two problems with this line of reasoning. The first is the assumption that "whatever is different is contrary." Two religious systems that differ in many respects need not be contrary in all respects. There is, in fact, significant overlap among the convictions of the great monotheistic religions of the world. Of course, it is also true that these religions have important differences and that some miracles may function to vindicate certain religious teachings over others. But as far as Hume has argued,

---

[34] In other words, this de jure objection to miracles cannot be settled without settling the de facto question about theism. For a similar response in the context of belief in God, see Plantinga (2000: 167–98).

God may have reasons for occasionally intervening on behalf of people from many different religious backgrounds. If, for example, he chooses to grant instantaneous healing to a Christian in one context and to a Muslim or a Hindu in another context, this hardly implies some thoroughgoing religious pluralism.

The second problem is that Hume simply assumes that miracle claims across different religions are always backed by evidence of the same quality. One need not grant this. For instance, Christians may contend that the evidence for Jesus' resurrection is better, for example, than the evidence that the Quran is a product of divine inspiration. Conversely, Muslims may argue that the divine origin of the Quran has higher-quality evidence in its favor than the resurrection. This is the point of departure into a healthy investigation of the facts. Hume's judgment that all religions are founded on miracles of equal evidential weight is too facile.

3.3 Conclusion

This section has addressed an epistemological objection to miracles that continues to have an enormous influence on contemporary thought. In my reconstruction, Hume's central thesis is that miracles are highly improbable events, and it is always more likely that miracle reports turn out to be false than that there be an exception to uniform human experience. This suggestion, however, is subject to counterexamples, such as the story of a prince who comes to believe in frozen rivers due to testimony. Hume tries to find a non-question-begging way around such counterexamples, but his attempts are unsuccessful.

As a result, we took a closer look at Hume's probabilistic judgments. Hume's skeptical project can be boiled down to two claims, namely (i) the prior probability of miracles is infinitesimally low and, (ii) the evidence in favor of miracle claims is always weak. I challenged both claims. The theist may contend that the prior probability of divine intervention, at least in some circumstances, may not be as low as the skeptic avers. I suggested, moreover, that Hume's cumulative case for (ii) is lackluster in each of its subparts.

The aim of this section has not been to argue for the veridicality of miracle claims either in general or in particular. Instead, I have only attempted to show that Hume's argument is not an insuperable problem for those who believe in miracles based on testimony. There is no simple way of discounting belief in miracles just because one arrives at them through the reports or witness of others. For a skeptical argument to succeed, one must deal with the facts: the quality and quantity of eyewitnesses, the naturalistic alternatives, and what one believes beforehand about the nature of God.

4 Biblical Miracles: Historiography and Significance

In Sections 1, 2, and 3, I examined and responded to a medley of theological, metaphysical, and epistemological objections against special divine actions. At the beginning of this Element, I also noted that although my defense of miracles applies to the great monotheistic religions of the world generally, my own research is rooted in the Christian worldview. Many of the examples I have already used reflect this fact. This section delves even deeper into the topic of miracles within the Christian context.

Many Christians claim to have witnessed, or at least know someone who has witnessed, some special divine act (see the Pew Research study cited in Section 3). However, at a more fundamental level, the truth of Christianity does not reside in contemporary miracles but rather in miracles that occurred in the past – at the inception of the Christian movement itself.[35] The most important miracle, of course, is the resurrection of Jesus. Without the resurrection, the foundation of Christianity melts away, and nothing remains except the unvindicated ramblings of a failed eschatological prophet. As Paul puts it, "If Christ has not been raised, your faith is futile, and you are still in your sins. Then those who have also died in Christ have perished. If for this life only we have hoped in Christ, we are of all people to be most pitied" (1 Cor. 15:17–19).

Besides the resurrection, the Christian scriptures also describe many other special divine acts. The Old Testament depicts burning bushes, divine plagues against Egypt, the parting of the Red Sea, the fall of Jericho's walls, and the pouring down of fire from heaven upon the prophets of Baal. In the New Testament, Jesus performs astonishing healings and exorcisms that draw large crowds. Similar divine power is eventually granted to Jesus' disciples, as described in the book of Acts.

Given the abundance of miracles in Scripture, it may come as some surprise that many biblical scholars do not believe that the veracity of miracles stories can be known or investigated historically. In the first part of this section, I address two reasons some New Testament historians consider miracle claims problematic. In the second part, I attempt to answer a different question: What is the *significance* of miracles? If there is a God who occasionally intervenes in our space-time realm, why does he do so? In other words, what function do miracles play? I provide several answers to this question within the context of Jesus' miracles in the Gospels.

---

[35] Indeed, contemporary Christians should be cautious about an over-fascination with miracles for their own sake (Mark 8:12; Luke 23:8–11) and not lose sight of the source and purpose of miracles.

4.1 Miracles and Biblical Scholarship

The current scholarly landscape regarding miracles in New Testament studies is intriguing. On the one hand, there is an overwhelming consensus, even among the most skeptical scholars, that Jesus' contemporaries regarded him as a miracle worker who performed exorcisms and healings (Blackburn 2011: 117). The sources attesting to this fact are diverse and widespread, coming from both friends and foes.[36] Indeed, the perception of Jesus as a miracle worker by his contemporaries is one of the most indubitable historical facts about him. John Meier makes this point forcefully: "Put dramatically but without too much exaggeration: if the miracle traditions from Jesus' public ministry were to be rejected *in toto* as unhistorical, so should every other Gospel tradition about him" (1994: 630).

On the other hand, however, many scholars avoid addressing the *truth* of the miracle stories themselves. There are numerous reasons for this posture. Some simply reject the possibility of miracles without justification.[37] Others, following Bultmann (whom I quoted in Section 2), declare that miracles are incompatible with the deliverances of the modern, scientific world.[38] Others offer Humean arguments for the conclusion that no belief in miracle can be justified through testimony.[39] I have already answered these types of objections in earlier sections, so I will not repeat them here.

Two other arguments, however, tend to appear in the context of biblical historiography. The first is that historians *as historians* cannot establish miracles because historical investigation must be empirically grounded. The second is that the biblical authors did not conceive of miracles as we have been describing them, namely as special acts of God beyond the capacities of natural entities. Imposing our definition on these ancient authors – the argument goes – is therefore anachronistic. I will examine and respond to both arguments.

---

[36] For example, the enemy charge that Jesus is empowered by Beelzebul (Mark 3:22–30/Matt. 22:22–32/Luke 11:14–23) presupposes that he is performing exorcisms. The accusation is unlikely to be a later story invented by Christians. Josephus, a non-Christian, probably refers to Jesus as a worker of marvelous deeds (*Ant.* 18.3.3). See Meier (1991: 61) for a reconstruction of the original, pre-interpolated text.

[37] John Dominic Crossan, for instance, simply *presumes* that Jesus could not perform healings (1995: 82). And he claims without justification, "I do not think that anyone, anywhere, at any time brings dead people back to life" (95).

[38] See also E. P. Sanders (1993: 143).

[39] In an influential New Testament introduction textbook, Bart Ehrman claims, "As events that defy all probability, miracles create an inescapable dilemma for historians. Since historians can only establish what probably happened in the past, and the chances of a miracle happening, by definition, are infinitesimally remote, historians can never demonstrate that a miracle *probably* happened" (2019: 243–4, italics his). This is an impoverished version of an already-poor Humean argument. At least the Scottish philosopher recognized that testimonial evidence could, in principle, override low prior probabilities.

4.1.1 The Empirical Constraint on Historical Investigation

According to the first objection, historians, as members of the broader discipline of history, must appeal exclusively to evidence that is, in principle, accessible to others. Miracles, however, are caused by God and are therefore off-limits to historical investigation. Meier, for instance, states:

> [I]t is inherently impossible for historians working with empirical evidence within the confines of their own discipline ever to make the positive judgment "God has directly acted here to accomplish something beyond all human power." The very wording of this statement shows that it is essentially *theo-logical* ... What evidence and criteria could justify a historian *as a historian* in reaching such a judgment? (1994: 513–14, italics in original)

Similarly, Robert Webb declares that

> the historian's descriptions and explanations of events and their proposed causes and effects must be open to verification by readers from observable data interpreted as evidence. Thus, there is a necessary empirical element to the historical method ... This observable data is open to all historians and their readers, for these observable data and their corresponding explanations exist within the physical, space-time universe. If a person with a theistic worldview were to propose divine causation for a particular human event, this theistic explanation is, by its very nature, an explanation of a different order. (2011: 80–1)

One will note that Meier and Webb are not suggesting that miracles did not happen or that we cannot accept them. Instead, they claim that *as historians,* we cannot conclude that "such-and-such a miracle occurred." Let us call this the "empirical constraint" on historical investigation. Miracles seem problematic because *God* is their cause, and God is beyond empirical verification. Therefore, concluding that a miracle has occurred would mean postulating an unverifiable cause of an event.

It seems to me that there are at least three postures one might take regarding this objection. The first is to grant the empirical constraint on historical investigation, but to claim that the inference to a miracle is made in one's capacity as a philosopher or theologian and is therefore unproblematic. In other words, one would accept that historical research is intrinsically limited to the empirical world, just like a metal detector is limited to detecting metal. Miracles may have occurred in the past, but the historian, working as a historian, is colorblind to them. So, one might opt to "play by the rules" as delineated by Meier and Webb.

I'm not entirely unsympathetic to this approach, but it has several question-able implications. For instance, notice that the term "observable" must be qualified as "observable *in principle*" since we do not observe historical events directly. But some miracles may satisfy this condition after all. In principle, events such as Jesus' healing a man with leprosy (Mark 1:40–1) and raising Lazarus from dead (John 11:28) are empirically observable, and Jesus is the clear cause of the miracles.[40] Some miracles, in other words, seem to satisfy the empirical constraint on historical investigation.

There may, however, be some miracles where the cause appears to be God directly, without any intermediary. Consider the case of the resurrection: Jesus was alive before the crucifixion; he died through crucifixion; around three days later, he was alive again. Here the miracle seems to involve a nonempirical cause with, in principle, empirically verifiable effects.

The question is whether the resurrection is an empirical event. Some theists do not think so.[41] One might wonder, however, if the objection is operating under a definition of "empirical" that is too restrictive. This leads to the second posture one might take with respect to the empirical constraint on history – understanding the term "empirical" in a way that includes special divine acts. Scientists often appeal to the existence of non-observable entities if the observable effects justify doing so. One position known as *entity realism* is the view that unobservable entities postulated by our best scientific theories exist. Candidates include electrons, other subatomic particles, magnetic fields, and black holes.

How do scientists gather evidence for such entities? According to one theory, if we are able to manipulate these unobservable entities in a way that produces observable phenomena, then we have strong reason to believe such entities exist (Hacking 1983). So, for instance, we can build "guns" that shoot these unobservable entities (electrons). My aim here isn't to defend entity realism against its anti-realist opponents. The point is simply that some scientists – especially those involved in theoretical physics – often have no qualms about postulating and even experimenting with non-observable entities. While there are obvious dissimilarities between God and electrons, we may still wonder why the proposition *electrons caused phenomenon X* is acceptable to the scientist, yet the proposition *God caused phenomenon Y* is unacceptable to the historian.[42]

---

[40] Of course, we may nuance our claim theologically – for example, that the power of God was operative through Jesus, or that because Jesus was God such power proceeded from his divine nature. All this, however, is secondary.

[41] Meier believes that although the resurrection was a "real" event, it was not a "historical" event: the resurrection did not happen in space-time, a necessary condition for an event to be historical (1991: 201). Indeed, Meier does not even classify the resurrection as a miracle (1994: 529). For a rebuttal, see Craig (2009). Meier's odd conclusion strikes me as, at least in part, the result of confused definitions.

[42] As a side note, although of course we cannot manipulate God in the same way we do electrons, there may be a conceptual parallel involving prayer: people ask God to intervene and, as a result, he sometimes does.

It strikes me that the empirical constraint on historical inquiry is most often not about observation at all. Instead, the real motive for appealing to empirical verification is the desire to implement *methodological naturalism*. Methodological naturalism is the position that scientific and historical investigation ought to proceed as if *metaphysical naturalism* were true. Metaphysical naturalism, in turn, is usually understood as the view that there is no God or anything remotely like God (i.e., no Cartesian souls, angels, ghosts), and by extension, that there are no acts of God. In the context of history, this means that one cannot appeal to causes beyond the natural world as explanations for historical phenomena.

It is important to note that the empirical constraint and methodological naturalism are not necessarily allied principles, despite often being treated as such. As previously noted, some miracles, such as instantaneous healings of terminal illnesses, are in principle empirically observable. Yet they would presumably be unacceptable to the methodological naturalist. Or consider the following three events: (1) Jesus was alive before the crucifixion, (2) he died on a cross, and (3) he was alive three days later. These too are, in principle, empirically observable. Yet it would be a strange methodological naturalist who affirmed the conjunction of (1), (2), and (3)![43]

In any case, a third option is to reject methodological naturalism (and the empirical constraint on history) wholesale. The reasons for adopting methodological naturalism usually boil down to two considerations. One argument, reminiscent of Hume, is that history is replete with miracles claims, and if one accepts some claims as historical, then one must accept them all. I have already addressed a version of this argument in Section 3. In short, we cannot simply assume that all miracle claims have equally strong evidence in their favor. This must be decided on a case-to-case basis.

The other prominent reason for accepting methodological naturalism is that history as a discipline must be collaborative, nondiscriminatory, and open to many religious viewpoints. Miracles would allegedly undermine this collaborative effort and are therefore off-limits to history *proper.* This argument, I think, assumes a more general and problematic principle, namely that if historians disagree strongly about some topic T, then in order to preserve collaboration and avoid discrimination, T should be off-limits to historical inquiry. Why not

---

[43] The methodological naturalist might respond that such instantaneous healings only *appeared* to occur, that Jesus only *appeared* to die, and that he was only *perceived* to be alive later (Johnson 2018: 569). But adding such qualifiers seems to be done only to keep the historian at an arm's distance away from miracle claims. To maintain consistency, one would have to qualify *all* empirical claims in this manner (e.g., that Caesar only *appeared* to cross the Rubicon, that George Washington was only *perceived* to be the first American president) – surely a mistaken result.

instead allow for investigation into T, allowing historians to form their own conclusions even if they disagree? Indeed, isn't the pursuit of truth *advanced* when historians examine evidence and challenge the assumptions and interpretations of others? It strikes me then, that this sort of consideration in favor of methodological naturalism is merely pragmatic.

In sum, when thinking about miracles and history, believers in miracles might take one of three postures. First, they might grant the empirical constraint on history and claim that beliefs in miracle are formed by philosophical inference from the historical data and are therefore legitimate and unproblematic. Second, believers might accept the empirical constraint on history but suggest that the concept of the "empirical" is broad enough to encompass causation by God, an unobserved entity, and that therefore miracles are within the scope of empirical investigation after all. Finally, they might simply reject the view that historical inquiry must be constrained empirically or that it must abide by the "rules" of methodological naturalism.

4.1.2 Miracles and Anachronism

Another argument that often appears in the context of biblical historiography is that it is anachronistic to impose our modern concept of miracles onto the biblical authors and their views about nature and miracles. David Aune, for instance, writes,

> In ancient Israelite and early Jewish tradition, there is no sharp distinction between the constant miraculous character of God's providence (Job 37:5–22) and the special mighty acts that God performs for his people. While miracles are special and exceptional, they are not "against nature," since there is no conception of "nature" in the Hebrew Bible. Neither is there a special term for "miracle" in Scripture, though there are "signs" . . . that is, extraordinary events through which people experience the sovereign power of God. (2010: 956)

There are at least two claims in this passage. The first is that the authors of the Old Testament and adjacent Jewish literature believed that there was no division between God's constant general providential activity, on the one hand, and his special acts, on the other. The second is that these ancient authors had no concept of "nature" and a fortiori no concept of miracles that go "against nature." Meier echoes this same idea: "Only the creative power of God, not 'natural' laws inherent in the realities of time and space, keeps the world from falling back into disorder. God gives or imposes laws on his creatures; those laws do not arise 'naturally' out of the creatures because of their very essence" (1994: 512–13).

I have several responses to this "argument from anachronism." First, we must be clear about definitions. In Section 2, I characterized miracles as events that "exceed" the capacities of natural entities, rather than as events that go "against" nature. Miracles, as instances of divine causation, do not go against nature any more than my lifting a book off a desk goes against nature. This understanding of miracles avoids any reference to "laws of nature" that govern the behavior of things in the world.

Second, if the argument aims to conclude that we and the ancients are *referring* to different things when we speak of miracles, then a proper theory of reference will avoid the problem. For example, the ancients also understood "light" and "water" differently than we do today. We now know that light is a certain visible range on the electromagnetic spectrum and that water is H_2O. The ancients, of course, did not know this. However, it does not follow that they and we are not referring to the same things. Scientific advances over time have informed and sharpened our understanding of light and water. Similarly, theological and philosophical reflection has also informed and sharpened our understanding of the essence of miracles. In other words, we can still refer successfully to the same phenomena under more nuanced descriptions.

Third, Aune seems to imply that the ancient Israelites lacked the concepts of nature or miracles, at least in part due to the absence of corresponding words in Hebrew. However, even though there is no direct Hebrew equivalent for the Greek term *physis* (usually translated as "nature"), it does not follow that the Hebrew speakers lacked the concept referred to by the term (Silva 2014: 631). For example, although there is no single Hebrew term in the Old Testament that corresponds to our word "adoption," the ancient authors still had a clear understanding of the concept (Friedeman 2020).

Fourth, in any case, this objection fails because the ancients did in fact have a robust concept of nature endowed by God with certain capacities. So, they could understand how God might act in ways that exceed these capacities. A full biblical theology of nature would go beyond the scope of this Element, but we will examine several important passages. The most relevant is the creation narrative in Genesis, which later authors in the Jewish tradition developed in their own contexts. In Genesis, we find not only the great act of creation but also God's bestowing capacities or powers upon created things. The most immediate capacity is the ability to reproduce:

> Then God said, "Let the earth put forth vegetation: plants yielding seed, and fruit trees of every kind on earth that bear fruit with the seed in it." And it was so. The earth brought forth vegetation: plants yielding seed of every kind, and trees of every kind bearing fruit with the seed in it. And God saw that it was good. (Gen. 1:11–12)

It is important to note that the *earth* produces vegetation, *plants* yield seed, and *trees* produce fruit. This capacity for independent reproduction does not exclude God's creative act. Instead, the two work in tandem. As Victor Hamilton explains, in this passage "the concept of both the supernatural and the natural have their place. What exists exists because of the creative word of God ... This spoken word grants the means of self-perpetuation to various species and orders of creation. Here then is both point and process, with neither eclipsing the other" (1990: 126). In other words, the creation narrative suggests that while all things ultimately derive from the creator, God has given his creatures certain inherent capacities.

Now, Aune cites Job 37:5–22 as a supporting passage. Here are some excerpts from those verses:

> God thunders wondrously with his voice; he does great things that we cannot comprehend. For to the snow he says, "Fall on the earth" ... By the breath of God, ice is given, and the broad waters are frozen fast. He loads the thick cloud with moisture; the clouds scatter his lightning. They turn round and round by his guidance ... Whether for correction, or for his land, or for love, he causes it to happen.

At first glance, it may seem that God is characterized as a direct cause of physical phenomena. However, we should be cautious when interpreting this (and similar) passages for two reasons. First, it isn't clear that the author of Job intends to provide a theology of nature, as the author of the opening chapters of Genesis does. Such descriptions of God in Job seem to advance the author's existential message rather than deliver a metaphysics of divine action.

Furthermore, other nearby passages seem to suggest, by contrast, that there are laws of nature that govern the universe. For example, in the very next chapter, God asks Job, "Do you determine the laws of the heaven? Can you establish their rule upon earth?" (38:25–6).[44] My claim is not that Job advocates either a law-based metaphysics or universal exclusive causation by God. Rather, I suggest that such matters are not the aim of the author of Job at all, and that therefore such passages should not be used as supporting evidence either way.[45]

---

[44] Translation from the *New English Translation* corresponding to that of David Clines (2015: 1050). See Clines (2015: 1115–16) on this passage.

[45] One can point to other passages that seem to express God's unilateral causation (e.g., Ps. 135:5–7, 147:15–18, Job 26:7–14), others that suggest the independent activity of natural things (e.g., Eccles. 1:5–7, Isa. 55:10–11, Ps. 148:3–6, Jer. 33:25–6), and others that seem to combine both (e.g., Ps. 104:10–14, Jer. 5:22). It appears that these passages are not intended to furnish a theology of divine action in any systematic fashion. However, it is possible that at least some of them laid the groundwork for later thinkers in the biblical intellectual tradition to adopt and develop metaphysical theories about nature and its governing principles. Many thanks to Eric Wagner for bringing this to my attention.

Fifth, as we draw closer to the time of the New Testament, we begin to see Jewish authors under Hellenistic influence describe the natural capacities of entities more explicitly. Consider two examples.[46] The author of the Wisdom of Solomon longs for the establishment of a new harmony in nature, where "[f]ire even in water retained its normal power, and water forgot its fire-quenching nature" (19:20). This passage explicitly mentions powers and essences attached to natural phenomena.

In one of his works, Philo of Alexandria discusses the different features that God has bestowed on physical bodies (*Deus.* 34–47 [Yonge]). He writes, "[F]or some bodies he has endowed with habit, others with nature, others with soul, and some with rational soul." Philo explains that some natural bodies have limited abilities: stones and beams have the power of "habit" because they are solid and retain their shape. Other entities are different. For example, God has "given to plants a nature which he has combined of as many powers as possible, that is, of the nutritive, and the changeable, and the forming power; for they are nourished when they have need of nourishment." Last, human beings have the power of intellect, which gives us freedom, a power that Philo calls "spontaneous will." In both the Wisdom of Solomon and Philo, therefore, we find a clear articulation that things in the world have powers or capacities.

In sum, I have suggested that even if our concept of nature and of miracles may not perfectly align with those of the ancients, we can still refer to the same phenomena. Additionally, I proposed that a robust concept of nature can be found both in the Old Testament and in Jewish literature approaching the time of the New Testament. Therefore, the charge of anachronism is unfounded.

4.2 The Significance of Miracles

In this final section, I wish to comment on the significance of miracles, including their function and meaning. Up to this point, our discussion, especially in Sections 1, 2, and 3, has addressed miracles in the abstract. However, it is important to note that miracles, taken in isolation, do not have any intrinsic meaning. For instance, suppose that God causes a giant waterfall to burst out of a large rock in the Sahara Desert. Such an event might strike us as wonderful and surprising. But there would be an additional question: *Why* did God perform this a miracle? What was the miracle's function? Answering these questions requires looking at the broader context in which the miracle occurred to uncover its meaning.

In the New Testament, there is no single Greek term that corresponds to the English word "miracle." English translations of the New Testament often use

---

[46] See Silva (2014: 630–4) for more examples.

the word "miracle" as a translation of three different Greek terms: *semeion* (sign), *teras* (wonder), and *dynamis* (power). Together, these words provide a rough description of miracles in the New Testament: they are wonderous displays of power that function as signs.

In what follows, I will elaborate on the significance of New Testament miracles, focusing specifically on the miracles of Jesus. Miracles serve at least four functions: (i) as signs of Jesus' identity, (ii) as acts of compassion, (iii) as inaugurating steps in the kingdom of God, and ultimately (iv) as a guarantor of future resurrection.

4.2.1 Signs of Jesus' Identity

The question "Who was Jesus?" defies a simple answer. The Gospels, in fact, can be seen as biographical attempts to answer this exact question.[47] Miracles play a significant role in this respect. In particular, they function to authenticate Jesus' identity.

In one passage, for example, the imprisoned John the Baptist sends his disciples to Jesus with an important question (Matt. 11:2–6/Luke 7:18–23). Here is Matthew's shorter version:

> When John heard in prison what the Messiah was doing, he sent word by his disciples and said to him, "Are you the one who is to come, or are we to wait for another?" Jesus answered them, "Go and tell John what you hear and see: the blind receive sight, the lame walk, the lepers are cleansed, the deaf hear, the dead are raised, and the poor have good news brought to them."

In this passage, John wants to know whether Jesus is the "one who is to come," that is, the Messiah. In effect, therefore, Jesus points to his own miracles as signs that he is indeed the one who is to come.[48]

Miracles also reveal Jesus' identity as the Son of Man who has the power to forgive sins. In Mark 2:1–12, a paralytic is lowered through the roof of a house where Jesus is teaching. Jesus declares to the paralytic, "Son, your sins are forgiven." This causes great consternation among some in the room who question how Jesus can forgive sins – the prerogative of God alone. He then asks:

> "Which is easier, to say to the paralytic, 'Your sins are forgiven,' or to say, 'Stand up and take your mat and walk?' But so that you may know that the Son of Man has authority on earth to forgive sins" – he said to the paralytic – "I say to you, stand up, take your mat and go to your home." And he stood up, and immediately took the mat and went out before all of them (Mark 2:9–12a).

---

[47] On the biographical nature of the Gospels, see Burridge (2018) and Keener (2019).

[48] For a study about the expectations that the Messiah would be a healer, see Novakovic 2019.

Now, the Jewish sacrificial system provided a means of forgiveness for sin, but this was to be done exclusively through a specific and detailed process in the Temple. So, Jesus' miraculous healing has dual implications beyond just the ability to heal someone. First, it establishes that he has the authority to forgive sins directly, bypassing traditional Temple proceedings (Collins 2004: 397). Second, the miracle authenticates his claim to be the Son of Man, alluding to the apocalyptic figure in Daniel 7:12–13 who is given dominion over the world by God.

In addition, miracles also function to establish Jesus as the one who is sent into the world by God and who shares in the identity of God himself. This is the central message of John's Gospel. On one occasion, some Jewish authorities gather around Jesus to ask him if he is the Messiah (John 10:24). Jesus affirms this, laments their disbelief, and adds an even more controversial self-proclamation: "The Father and I are one" (10:30). At this, his interlocutors pick up stones to kill him. Jesus defends himself by appealing to the "good works" or miracles he has accomplished:

> Jesus replied, "I have shown you many good works from the Father. For which of these are you going to stone me? . . . If I am not doing the works of my Father, then do not believe me. But if I do them, even though you do not believe me, believe the works, so that you may know and understand that the Father is in me and I am in the Father." (10:31, 37–8).

The works that Jesus performed, referring to his miracles, are therefore Jesus' apologetic in favor of his claim to Messiahship and, more deeply, to his intimate and unique relationship with the Father.

4.2.2 Compassion

Another function of miracles is the simple act of compassion on behalf of Jesus toward the hopeless and disconsolate. Consider the following examples.

When Jesus visits a town called Nain, he sees a funeral procession for a widow who has lost her only son. In that ancient culture, women whose husbands and sons had died faced a bleak future, often relegated to a life of poverty and hardship at the bottom of the social hierarchy. Moved with compassion, Jesus tells the widow not to weep, and he brings her son back to life (Luke 7:13–15).

On another occasion, thousands of people follow Jesus to hear him teach. After three days, they have had nothing to eat, and Jesus knows that if he were to send them back home, they would faint along the way. Feeling compassion for the crowd, he miraculously feeds them using only seven loaves of bread and two fish (Mark 8:10).

According to another story, Jesus is leaving Jericho when two blind men cry out, "Lord, have mercy on us, Son of David." And even though the crowd attempts to silence them, Jesus, moved with compassion, touches their eyes and heals them (Matt. 20:30–4).

There are many more examples like these. These passages contain the Greek verb *splagchnizomai*, which is often translated as "to have compassion" in English. However, the word carries connotations that go beyond simple pity or caring. The Greek verb is derived from the noun *splagchnon*, meaning "bowels" – what today we would regard as the "gut" – which was regarded as the seat of love, pity, and sympathy. So, the Greek term conveys the idea of a deep, visceral, inwardly felt compassion. Miracles, therefore, also function to highlight Jesus' kindheartedness.

4.2.3 Inaugurating the Kingdom of God

Over the past century, many historical Jesus scholars have emphasized that one of Jesus' central messages was the arrival of the kingdom of God, and that Jesus saw himself at the center of its inauguration (Wright 1997: 198–319; Allison 1998). This message was manifested not only in Jesus' actions, teachings, and parables, but also as the purpose of some of his miracles.

In a passage we have already seen (Matt. 11:2–6), John the Baptist's disciples ask Jesus if he is the "one who is to come." Jesus answers affirmatively, pointing to his miracles as evidence. It is also important to note the kinds of miracles he mentions: "the blind receive sight, the lame walk, the lepers are cleansed, the deaf hear, the dead are raised, and the poor have good news brought to them." These sorts of miracles are allusions to Old Testament prophecies about the future restoration of Israel and the kingdom of God. For instance:

> Then the eyes of the blind shall be opened, and the ears of the deaf unstopped; then the lame shall leap like a deer, and the tongue of the speechless sing for joy. (Isa. 35:5–6)

> Your dead shall live, their corpses shall rise. O dwellers in the dust, awake and sing for joy! For your dew is a radiant dew, and the earth will give birth to those long dead. (Isa. 26:19)

> The Lord opens the eyes of the blind. The Lord lifts up those who are bowed down; the Lord loves the righteous . . . The Lord will reign forever, your God, O Zion, for all generations. (Ps. 146:8)

In essence, Jesus' response to John's disciples reveals that his miracles are not just signs that he is the Messiah: they also indicate that the fulfillment of Old

Testament prophecies is unfolding before their eyes and, as a result, the kingdom of God is imminent.

The connection between miracles and the kingdom is even more apparent in the context of Jesus' exorcism of a demon-possessed man who is blind and mute. In Matthew's account, the Pharisees accuse Jesus of casting out demons only by the power of Beelzebul, the ruler of the demons. Jesus replies:

> Every kingdom divided against itself is laid waste, and no city or house divided against itself will stand. If Satan casts out Satan, he is divided against himself; how then will his kingdom stand? . . . But if it is by the Spirit of God that I cast out demons, then the kingdom of God has come to you. (Matt. 22:25–6, 28).

In other words, exorcisms themselves demonstrate that the kingdom of God has arrived through the decisive acts of Jesus.

We can see, therefore, that Jesus' miracles were closely connected to his message about the inauguration of the kingdom of God and his central role in it. According to Graham Twelftree, "the miracles are themselves, the eschatological kingdom of God in operation or made manifest" (2011: 2542).

4.2.4 Hope for Future Resurrection

Jesus' resurrection is the miracle par excellence. While its significance is multifaceted, two points stand out. The first is that the resurrection vindicates Jesus against the accusations for which he was crucified. In the eyes of those who condemned him, Jesus was a both a false prophet leading Israel away from God, and a blasphemer for his radical self-proclamations. The resurrection, however, functioned as a divine confirmation that Jesus was who he said he was.

Second, the resurrection carries a further implication for Christians, namely the hope of a future resurrection and eternal life in the presence of God himself. During the first century, there were varying Jewish beliefs about what happened after death. The Sadducees, for instance, believed that there was no afterlife or resurrection. The most popular view, however, was that there would be a universal bodily resurrection at the end of the age, when God would judge the both the righteous and the unrighteous (Wright 2003). Against this backdrop, Paul writes the following in his first letter to the Corinthians:

> Now if Christ is proclaimed as raised from the dead, how can some of you say there is no resurrection of the dead? . . . For if the dead are not raised, then Christ has not been raised. If Christ has not been raised, your faith is futile, and you are still in your sins. Then those also who have died in Christ have perished . . . But in fact Christ has been raised from the dead, the first fruits of those who have died. For since death came through a human being, the resurrection of the dead has also come through a human being. (1 Cor. 15:12, 16–21)

Here Paul uses Jesus' resurrection as proof that there is such a thing as resurrection from the dead. Jesus is the "first fruits" – the preview, so to speak – of what the later general resurrection will be like. Those who are "in Christ" have a proof by demonstration that death is not the end.

In his first letter to the Thessalonians, Paul notes that the resurrection will involve a reunion with loved ones:

> But we do not want you to be uninformed, brothers and sisters, about those who have died, so that you may not grieve as others do who have no hope. For since we believe that Jesus died and rose again, even so, through Jesus, God will bring with him those who have died . . . and so we will be with the Lord forever. (1 Thess. 4:13–14, 17b)

The hope of being reunited with those who have passed away does not diminish grief in this life. Rather, says Paul, it provides a different texture to grief since death is not permanent. So, Jesus' resurrection, the decisive miracle, is also the ultimate sign. It anticipates the defeat of death itself, gives the believers hope of being united with loved ones beyond the grave, and foretells an endless future in the presence of God.

4.3 Conclusion

The aim of this Element has been to explore some of the questions and "problems" that arise when reflecting upon God's action in the world. We began by distinguishing miracles from God's initial act of creation, his conserving the universe in being, and his concurrence with the activities of created beings. The rest of Section 1 developed and responded to various theological objections to miracles. If God exists and has the properties typically attributed to him by the world's monotheistic religions, then there is no persuasive theological reason for thinking that he couldn't intervene in the world he has created.

In Section 2, I defended the possibility of miracles against metaphysical objections that often arise in the context of scientific discourse. These objections usually allege that miracles violate some important principle – for example, the causal closure of the physical or the conservation of energy. I showed that these principles are no obstacle to miracles; either the principles are false, or they don't apply to divine intervention. Moreover, the common objection that miracles violate laws of nature is ambiguous because there are many metaphysical models of the laws of nature. I therefore examined five such models and demonstrated that the objection fails on all of them.

Section 3 addressed Hume's famous epistemological objection to miracles, namely that one is never rationally justified in believing miracles on the basis of testimony. Central to his argument are the convictions that (i) miracles are intrinsically improbable events, and that (ii) testimonial evidence is never strong enough to overcome this great improbability. I presented two reasons why the prior probability of a miracle may not be as low as Hume supposed. Moreover, upon closer inspection, his attempts to downplay the strength of testimonial evidence are weak. Despite its enormous influence, Hume's argument is deficient.

In this final section, I focused specifically on miracles in the Christian tradition. Some biblical scholars maintain that although miracles may have occurred in the past, a historian *as a historian* cannot arrive at such a conclusion. It is not clear, however, that Christians must accept this empirical constraint on historical investigation, and even if they do, the objector may be using a definition of "empirical" that is unacceptably narrow. Other biblical scholars argue the ancient Jewish authors thought of nature and miracles differently than we moderns do and that imposing our concepts on them is anachronistic. I suggested, however, that ancient Jewish authors did, in fact, possess a robust concept of nature and special divine acts, such that referring to them today is unproblematic.

In the second part of this section, I reflected on the significance of miracles in the New Testament. Jesus' miracles authenticated his proclamations about himself, namely that he was the Messiah, the Son of Man who was able to forgive sins, and that he was sent by the Father. They also exhibited Jesus' deep-seated compassion, especially toward the weak, sick, and vulnerable. Most importantly, the resurrection demonstrated that God had vindicated the actions, life, and teachings of this man from Nazareth. Jesus' resurrection functions as a guarantor of a future in which death is defeated, loved ones are reunited, and God's kingdom is fully established.

References

Allison, Dale C., Jr. (1998). *Jesus of Nazareth: Millenarian Prophet.* Minneapolis, MN: Fortress Press.

Allison, Dale C., Jr. (2021). *The Resurrection of Jesus: Apologetics, Polemics, History.* London: Bloomsbury.

Alston, William P. (1986). Does God Have Beliefs? *Religious Studies*, 22(3/4), 287–306.

Aquinas, Thomas (1956). *On the Truth of the Catholic Faith: Summa Contra Gentiles Book Three: Providence Part 2.* Vernon J. Bourke, trans. Garden City, NJ: Images Books: Doubleday & Company, Inc.

Archer, Joel (2015). Against Miracles As Law-Violations: A Neo-Aristotelian Approach. *European Journal for Philosophy of Religion*, 7(4), 83–98.

Armstrong, David M. (1997). *A World of States of Affairs.* Cambridge: Cambridge University Press.

Armstrong, David M. (1983). *What Is a Law of Nature?* Cambridge: Cambridge University Press.

Audi, Paul (2011). Primitive Causal Relations and the Pairing Problem. *Ratio*, 24(1), 1–16.

Augustine (2012). *The Confessions, Part I.* 2nd ed., John. E. Rotelle, ed., Maria Boulding, trans. Hyde Park, NY: New City Press.

Aune, David E. (2010). Miracles and Miracle Workers. In John J. Collins and Daniel C. Harlow, eds., *The Eerdmans Dictionary of Early Judaism.* Grand Rapids, MI: Eerdmans, 956–8.

Bailey, Andrew M., Joshua Rasmussen, and Luke Van Horn (2011). No Pairing Problem. *Philosophical Studies*, 154(3), 349–60.

Basinger, David (2018). *Miracles.* Cambridge: Cambridge University Press.

Bauckham, Richard (2008). *Jesus and the God of Israel: God Crucified and Other Studies on the New Testament's Christology of Divine Identity.* Grand Rapids, MI: Eerdmans.

Bergmann, Michael (2001). Skeptical Theism and Rowe's New Evidential Argument from Evil. *Noûs*, 35(2), 278–96.

Bird, Alexander (2010). *Nature's Metaphysics: Laws and Properties.* Oxford: Oxford University Press.

Blackburn, Barry (2011). The Miracles of Jesus. In Graham. H. Twelftree, ed., *The Cambridge Companion to Miracles.* Cambridge: Cambridge University Press, 113–30.

Buckareff, Andrei (2016). Theological Realism, Divine Action, and Divine Location. In Andrei Buckareff and Yujin Nagasawa, eds., *Alternative Concepts of God: Essays on the Metaphysics of the Divine*. Oxford: Oxford University Press, 213–32.

Bultmann, Rudolf (1989). *The New Testament and Mythology and Other Basic Writings*. Shubert M. Ogden, trans. Philadelphia, PA: Fortress Press.

Burridge, Richard A. (2018). *What Are the Gospels? A Comparison with Graeco-Roman Biography*. Twenty-fifth anniversary ed. Waco, TX: Baylor University Press.

Clayton, Philip (2008). *Adventures in the Spirit: God, World, Divine Action*. Philadelphia, PA: Fortress Press.

Clines, David J. A. (2015). *Job 38–42, Volume 18B*. Nashville, TN: Thomas Nelson.

Collins, Adela Y. (2004). The Charge of Blasphemy in Mark 14.64. *Journal for the Study of the New Testament*, 26(4), 379–401.

Craig, William L. (1989). *Assessing the New Testament Evidence for the Historicity of the Resurrection of Jesus*. New York: Edwin Mellen Press.

Craig, William L. (2009). "Noli Me Tangere": Why John Meier Won't Touch the Risen Lord. *Heythrop Journal*, 50(1), 91–7.

Craig, William L., and James D. Sinclair (2009). The Kalam Cosmological Argument. In William L. Craig and James P. Moreland, eds., *The Blackwell Companion to Natural Theology*. Chichester: Wiley-Blackwell, 101–201.

Crossan, John D. (1995). *Jesus: A Revolutionary Biography*. San Francisco: HarperCollins.

Earman, John (2000). *Hume's Abject Failure: The Argument against Miracles*. Oxford: Oxford University Press.

Edwards, Denis (2010). *How God Acts: Creation, Redemption, and Special Divine Action*. Minneapolis, MN: Fortress Press.

Ehrman, Bart D. (2019). *The New Testament: A Historical Introduction to the Early Christian Writings*. 4th ed. New York: Oxford University Press.

Ellis, Brian (2002). *The Philosophy of Nature: A Guide to the New Essentialism*. Montreal: McGill-Queen's University Press.

Ellis, George (2000). Ordinary and Extraordinary Divine Action. In Robert J. Russell, Nancey Murphy, and Arthur Peacocke, eds., *Chaos and Complexity: Scientific Perspectives on Divine Action*. Vatican City: Vatican Observatory Publications.

Ellis, George (1999). The Theology of the Anthropic Principle. In Robert J. Russell, Nancey Murphy, and Cristopher. J. Isham, eds., *Quantum Cosmology and the Laws of Nature*. Vatican City: Vatican Observatory Publications.

Fales, Evan (2010). *Divine Intervention: Metaphysical and Epistemological Puzzles*. New York: Routledge.

Friedeman, Caleb T. (2020). Jesus' Davidic Lineage and the Case for Jewish Adoption. *New Testament Studies*, 66(2), 249–67.

Frost, Gloria (2014). Peter Olivi's Rejection of God's Concurrence with Created Causes. *British Journal for the History of Philosophy*, 22(4), 655–79.

Ganssle, Gregory (2021). Divine Causation and the Pairing Problem. In Gregory Ganssle, ed., *Philosophical Essays on Divine Causation*. New York: Routledge, 268–83.

Göcke, Benedikt P. (2015). The Many Problems of Special Divine Action. *European Journal for Philosophy of Religion*, 7(4), 23–36.

Hacking, Ian (1983). *Representing and Intervening: Introductory Topics in the Philosophy of Natural Science*. Cambridge: Cambridge University Press.

Hamilton, Victor P. (1990). *The Book of Genesis Chapters 1–17*. Grand Rapids, MI: Eerdmans.

Hasker, William (1999). *The Emergent Self*. Ithaca, NY: Cornell University Press.

Hughes, Christopher, and Robert M. Adams (1992). Miracles, Laws of Nature and Causation. *Proceedings of the Aristotelian Society, Supplementary Volumes*, 66, 179–224.

Hume, David (2007). *An Enquiry concerning Human Understanding*. Peter Millican, trans. Oxford: Oxford University Press.

Ivanova, Milena, and Steven French, eds. (2022). *The Aesthetics of Science*. London: Routledge.

Jaffe, Robert L., and Washington Taylor (2018). *The Physics of Energy*. Cambridge: Cambridge University Press.

Johnson, Luke T. (2018). *Miracles: God's Presence and Power in Creation*. Louisville, KY: Westminster John Knox Press.

Keener, Craig S. (2011). *Miracles: The Credibility of the New Testament Accounts*. 2 vols. Grand Rapids, MI: Baker Academic.

Keener, Craig S. (2019). *Christobiography: Memory, History, and the Reliability of the Gospels*. Grand Rapids, MI: Eerdmans.

Kim, Jaegwon (2007). *Physicalism, or Something Near Enough*. Princeton, NJ: Princeton University Press.

Kittle, Simon (2022). God Is (Probably) a Cause among Causes: Why the Primary/Secondary Cause Distinction Doesn't Help in Developing Non-interventionist Accounts of Special Divine Action. *Theology and Science*, 20(2), 247–62.

Larmer, Robert A. (2013). *The Legitimacy of Miracle*. Lanham, MD: Lexington Books.

Larmer, Robert A. (2014). Divine Intervention and the Conservation of Energy: A Reply to Evan Fales. *International Journal for Philosophy of Religion*, 75(1), 27–38.

Larmer, Robert A. (2021). Defending Special Divine Acts. In Gregory Ganssle, ed., *Philosophical Essays on Divine Causation*. New York: Routledge, 174–95.

Lewis, David (1973). *Counterfactuals*. Cambridge, MA: Harvard University Press.

Lewis, David (1986). *Philosophical Papers: Volume II*. New York: Oxford University Press.

Lewis, David (1997). Finkish Dispositions. *Philosophical Quarterly*, 47(187), 143–58.

Licona, Michael R. (2010). *The Resurrection of Jesus: A New Historiographical Approach*. Nottingham: IVP Academic.

Lindars, Barnabas (1986). Jesus Risen: Bodily Resurrection But No Empty Tomb. *Theology*, 89(728), 90–6.

Lord, Walter (2017). *The Miracle of Dunkirk: The True Story of Operation Dynamo*. New York: Open Road Media.

Lowe, E. J. (2008). *Personal Agency: The Metaphysics of Mind and Action*. Oxford: Oxford University Press.

Luck, Morgan (2016). Defining Miracles: Direct vs. Indirect Causation. *Philosophy Compass*, 11(5), 267–76.

Mackie, J. L. (1983). *The Miracle of Theism: Arguments for and against the Existence of God*. Oxford: New York: Oxford University Press.

McGrew, Timothy (2014). Miracles. In Edward N. Zalta, ed., *Stanford Encyclopedia of Philosophy*. [online]. http://plato.stanford.edu/archives/win2014/entries/miracles [Accessed April 28, 2015].

Meier, John P. (1991). *A Marginal Jew: Rethinking the Historical Jesus, Volume I: The Roots of the Problem and the Person*. New Haven, CT: Yale University Press.

Meier, John P. (1994). *A Marginal Jew: Rethinking the Historical Jesus, Volume II: Mentor, Message, and Miracles*. New Haven, CT: Yale University Press.

Menuge, Angus J. L., Jonathan J. Loose, and James P. Moreland, eds. (2018). *The Blackwell Companion to Substance Dualism*. Oxford: John Wiley & Sons.

Montero, Barbara (2003). Varieties of Causal Closure. In Sven Walter and Heinz-Dieter Heckmann, eds., *Physicalism and Mental Causation*. Exeter: Imprint Academic, 173–87.

Morgan, Thomas (1741). *Physico-theology: Or, A Philosophico-Moral Disquisition concerning Human Nature, Free Agency, Moral Government, and Divine Providence*. London: Printed for the author.

Mumford, Stephen (2001). Miracles: Metaphysics and Modality. *Religious Studies*, 37(2), 191–202.

Mumford, Stephen (2004). *Laws in Nature*. Oxford: Routledge.

Murphy, Nancy (2000). Ordinary and Extraordinary Divine Action. In Robert. J. Russell, Nancey Murphy, and Arthur Peacocke, eds., *Chaos and Complexity: Scientific Perspectives on Divine Action*. Vatican City: Vatican Observatory Publications, 325–57.

Novakovic, Lidija (2019). *Messiah, the Healer of the Sick: A Study of Jesus As the Son of David in the Gospel of Matthew*. Tubingen: Mohr Siebeck.

Oord, Thomas J. (2010). *The Nature of Love: A Theology*. St. Louis, MO: Chalice Press.

Oord, Thomas J. (2015). *The Uncontrolling Love of God: An Open and Relational Account of Providence*. Downers Grove, IL: IVP Academic.

Overall, Christine (2014). Reply to "Overall and Larmer on Miracles As Evidence for the Existence of God." *Dialogue: Canadian Philosophical Review / Revue canadienne de philosophie*, 53(4), 601–9.

Papineau, David (2007). The Rise of Physicalism. In Carl Gillett and Barry Loewer, eds., *Physicalism and Its Discontents*. Cambridge: Cambridge University Press, 3–36.

Peterson, Michael L. (2022). *Monotheism, Suffering, and Evil*. Cambridge: Cambridge University Press.

Peterson, Michael L., William Hasker, Bruce Reichenbach, and David Basinger (2013). *Reason & Religious Belief: An Introduction to the Philosophy of Religion*. 5th ed. New York: Oxford University Press.

Pew Research Center (2006). *Spirit and Power: A 10-Country Survey of Pentecostals* [online]. www.pewresearch.org/religion/2006/10/05/spirit-and-power [Accessed February 1, 2023].

Philo (1993). *The Works of Philo: Complete and Unabridged, New Updated Edition*. C. D. Yonge, trans. Peabody, MA: Hendrickson.

Plantinga, Alvin (1989). *God, Freedom, and Evil*. Grand Rapids, MI: Eerdmans.

Plantinga, Alvin (2000). *Warranted Christian Belief*. New York: Oxford University Press.

Plantinga, Alvin (2008). What Is "Intervention"? *Theology and Science*, 6(4), 369–401.

Plantinga, Alvin (2011). *Where the Conflict Really Lies: Science, Religion, and Naturalism*. New York: Oxford University Press.

Popper, Karl R. (1992). *The Logic of Scientific Discovery*. New York: Routledge.

Quinn, Philip (1988). Divine Conservation, Secondary Causes, and Occasionalism. In Thomas V. Morris, ed., *Divine and Human Action*. Ithaca, NY: Cornell University Press, 50–73.

Ramsey, Frank P. (1990). Universals of Law and of Fact (1928). In D. H. Mellor, ed., *F. P. Ramsey: Philosophical Papers*. Cambridge: Cambridge University Press, 140–4.

Rota, Gian-Carlo (1997). The Phenomenology of Mathematical Beauty. *Synthese*, 111(2), 171–82.

Russell, Robert J. (2008). *Cosmology: From Alpha to Omega. The Creative Mutual Interaction of Theology and Science*. Minneapolis, MN: Fortress Press.

Sanders, Ed P. (1993). *The Historical Figure of Jesus*. New York: Penguin Books.

Seeskin, Kenneth (2011). Miracles in Jewish Philosophy. In Graham H. Twelftree, ed., *The Cambridge Companion to Miracles*. Cambridge: Cambridge University Press, 254–70.

Silva, Ignacio A. (2015). A Cause among Causes? God Acting in the Natural World. *European Journal for Philosophy of Religion*, 7(4), 99–114.

Silva, Ignacio A. (2022). *Providence and Science in a World of Contingency: Thomas Aquinas' Metaphysics of Divine Action*. Abingdon: Routledge.

Silva, Moises, ed. (2014). *New International Dictionary of New Testament Theology and Exegesis Set*. Revised ed. Grand Rapids, MI: Zondervan Academic.

Stoeger, William R. (2009). Describing God's Action in the World in Light of Scientific Knowledge of Reality. In Leron F. Shults, Nancey C. Murphy, and Robert J. Russell, eds., *Philosophy, Science and Divine Action*. Leiden: Brill, 111–39.

Stump, Eleonore (1995). Non-Cartesian Substance Dualism and Materialism without Reductionism. *Faith and Philosophy*, 12(4), 505–31.

Stump, Eleonore (2003). *Aquinas*. London: Routledge.

Stump, Eleonore (2012). *Wandering in Darkness: Narrative and the Problem of Suffering*. Oxford: Oxford University Press.

Suárez, Francisco (2002). *On Creation, Conservation, and Concurrence: Metaphysical Disputations 20–22*. Alfred J. Freddoso, trans. South Bend, IN: St. Augustine's Press.

Swinburne, Richard (1970). *The Concept of Miracle*. London: Palgrave Macmillan.

Swinburne, Richard (2003). *The Resurrection of God Incarnate*. Oxford: Clarendon.

Talim, Meena (2002). Buddha and Miracles. *Bulletin of the Deccan College Research Institute*, 62/63, 249–63.

Thomas, David (2011). Miracles in Islam. In Graham H. Twelftree, ed., *The Cambridge Companion to Miracles*. Cambridge: Cambridge University Press, 199–215.

Tillich, Paul (1953). *Systematic Theology*. London: Nisbet.

Tooley, Michael (1987). *Causation: A Realist Approach*. Oxford: Clarendon.

Tooley, Michael (1997). *Time, Tense, and Causation*. Oxford: Clarendon.

Twelftree, Graham H. (2011). The Message of Jesus I: Miracles, Continuing Controversies. In Thomas Holmén and Stanley E. Porter, eds., *Handbook for the Study of the Historical Jesus*. Leiden: Brill, 2517–48.

Van Inwagen, Peter (2008). *The Problem of Evil*. Oxford: Oxford University Press.

Vander Laan, David (2022). Creation and Conservation. In Edward N. Zalta, ed., *Stanford Encyclopedia of Philosophy*. Stanford, CA: Metaphysics Research Lab, Stanford University. https://plato.stanford.edu/entries/creation-conservation.

Von Wachter, Daniel (2015). Miracles Are Not Violations of the Laws of Nature Because the Laws Do Not Entail Regularities. *European Journal for Philosophy of Religion*, 7(4), 37–60.

Webb, Robert L. (2011). "The Rules of the Game: History and Historical Method in the Context of Faith. The Via Media of Methodological Naturalism." *Journal for the Study of the Historical Jesus*, 9 (1), 59–84.

Wright, N. T. (1997). *Jesus and the Victory of God*. Minneapolis, MN: Fortress Press.

Wright, N. T. (2003). *The Resurrection of the Son of God*. Minneapolis, MN: Fortress Press.

Acknowledgments

Many thanks to Vince Archer, Caleb Friedeman, Greg Ganssle, Bob Hartman, Robert Larmer, Jimmy Myers, Mike Peterson, and Eric Wagner for looking at drafts of this Element. I am also grateful for feedback from audiences at the American Philosophical Association Pacific Division and the Saint Louis University Biblical Studies Workshop.

Cambridge Elements ☰

The Problems of God

Elements in the Series

A full series listing is available at: www.cambridge.org/EPOG